# VENICE PRESERVED

# VEN

Photographs by
Jorge Lewinski and Mayotte Magnus

# ICE PRESERVED

Introduction by John Julius Norwich
Text by Peter Lauritzen

ADLER & ADLER

To future generations in Venice

Published in the United States in 1986 by
Adler & Adler, Publishers, Inc.
4550 Montgomery Avenue
Bethesda, Maryland 20814

Originally published in Great Britain by
Michael Joseph Ltd.

Library of Congress Catalog Card Number: 86–50108

ISBN 0–917561–17–1

Printed and bound in Italy by Arnoldo Mondadori

# Contents

Acknowledgements                                    vi

Author's Note                                       vii

Introduction by John Julius Norwich               1

VENICE SUBMERGED                                   23

DYING VENICE                                        36

THE TWENTIETH-CENTURY SIEGE                        51

UNDERMINING THE LAST DEFENCES                      60

RELIEF: PAINTINGS RESTORED                         74

RELIEF: CHURCHES REPAIRED                          93

RELIEF: STONEWORK CONSERVED                       105

THE TRIUMPH OF THE GOLDEN HORSES                  118

BUILDING FOR THE FUTURE                           127

VENICE'S LAGOON                                    150

VENETIAN LIFE ENRICHED                            161

Index                                             174

# Acknowledgements

There is hardly space enough in the whole of this book to acknowledge everyone who, over the past two decades, has contributed to my understanding and appreciation of conservation and restoration work in Venice. In fact, I have tried to avoid overburdening my account with the names of all the people concerned in the sundry phases of various individual restoration projects. From my point of view, foreign fundraisers; local patriots, enthusiasts and polemicists; government ministers and politicians; art historians, scientists and restorers; administrative authorities and bureaucrats both past and present; as well as a host of skilled craftsmen, workmen and technicians all deserve individual mention, but for the purpose of producing this particular work, the photographers and I would like to acknowledge our debt of gratitude to baronessa Maria Teresa Rubin de Cervin Albrizzi, directress of UNESCO's Venice office; to Professore Francesco Valcanover, Sovrintendente ai Beni Artistici e Storici di Venezia; and to Signor Giandomenico Romanelli, Direttore ai Civici Musei di Venezia.

# Author's Note

MY OWN ACQUAINTANCE WITH THE PROJECT to preserve Venice dates back to the events of 4 November 1966, which also brought me firsthand experience of the havoc flood waters can wreak. I was living in Florence when the terrible flood struck, inundating the dining-room, kitchen and sitting-room of my house with five and a half feet of fuel oil soaked water. By sheer accident, I happened to be away from Florence that day and, during the previous week, had been in Vicenza staying with a friend. We decided to drive over to Venice for a late lunch and, suspecting nothing at all, we boarded what proved to be the last *vaporetto* allowed to circulate in the Grand Canal on that November Saturday afternoon. Of course, we missed our lunch in Venice because the city was in the throes of the most severe *acqua alta* in this century's history. Perhaps it was fate that two such calamities should change my life and find me, a year later, moving to Venice where I have lived ever since.

I did not come to Venice to help restore her paintings or monuments. I moved there because her beauty and her wonderful sea-girt isolation were irresistible to me. Her past power and glory eventually held me enthralled and, in a number of books, I attempted to puzzle out the amazing story of her great gifts to our civilization. In the course of my studies, I was asked by UNESCO's Venice office to prepare a second, enlarged edition of their brief catalogue of all the restoration carried out since 1966 by the thirty or so international committees organized to restore and protect Venetian monuments and works of art. This catalogue, *Venice Restored/Venise Restaurée*, told only a limited part of the story. Now at long last, the Superintendency of the Artistic and Historic Heritage and the Superintendency of the Architectural Heritage and the Environment – referred to throughout my essay by their simpler, earlier designations as the Superintendent of the Galleries and the Superintendent of Monuments – have decided to publish a fuller account: a complete catalogue of all the restoration work that has come under their jurisdiction in the past twenty years.

But the long and fascinating tale of cleaning paintings, repairing buildings and restoring statuary since 1966 is still only part of the story. And so, when I was approached by Jorge and

# AUTHOR'S NOTE

Mayotte Lewinski with their proposal to record what has been and is being done in Venice in the way of restoration work, and by John Julius Norwich who agreed to write an introduction for us and appealed to my love of history by suggesting we reuse Thomas Otway's fine title for our book, I was delighted to join so distinguished a team. I have taken this opportunity to tell the story of Venice's preservation from the Venetian point of view – or at least from the point of view of an historian who has lived in Venice for twenty years and who has tried to understand both the Venice of the past and the Venice of today. The reader should expect to find an explanation of why so much needed to be done for Venice and what the results have been, both positive and negative. The future is, of course, open to question, although our choice of title is as much an act of faith as it is a summary of achievement.

P.L.L.
La Festa del Redentore
Venice, 1985

# Introduction

'STREETS FULL OF WATER PLEASE ADVISE' – Robert Benchley's famous telegram, despatched on his first arrival in the city, sums up nearly everybody's immediate reaction to the mention of the word 'Venice' – the fact that, as Browning had put it the best part of a century before, 'the sea's a street there'. And, of course, it is perfectly true. But that is only the beginning of the Venetian miracle. Venice is not just the only major city in the world that happens to use water in the way other cities use concrete; nor is she simply the most beautiful one. She can also claim to have been an independent republic for over a thousand years – a period of time comfortably longer than that which separates us from William the Conqueror – for several centuries of which she was the acknowledged mistress of the Mediterranean, the richest and most powerful state in Europe. Moreover, throughout that millennium her government continued stable and uninterrupted, with Doge succeeding Doge in smooth and unbroken succession (though one, admittedly, was executed) and with only a single, very minor revolt – by a handful of discontented young aristocrats – which was put down in a few hours, thanks largely to the presence of mind of one old lady.

And all this, let it never be forgotten, was achieved by a city that began its history under the most unfavourable and unpropitious auspices that can possibly be imagined: as a funk-hole. Why, you may ask, *why* would anyone in their senses dream of building even a village – let alone a great European capital – on a cluster of shallow sand-banks set in the middle of a malarial and malodorous lagoon? Yet this is precisely what those early Venetians did, and they did so for the most persuasive reason of all. They were terrified. Early in the fifth century, when the barbarian hordes had begun sweeping down from central Europe, looting and pillaging, burning and ravaging all the rich imperial cities of north-east Italy, those sand-banks represented safety; and although in the early years the fleeing populations may have looked upon them as temporary places of refuge only, conditions on the mainland soon obliged them to accept the lagoon as their permanent home.

Their descendants have never ceased to bless the day that they did so. Those two and a half miles of shallow water – always a far more effective protection than deep – that cut them off

1

from the *terra firma* were to shape not just the whole character of Venice, but her whole future as well. First of all, they were to offer her a degree of security unknown anywhere else in Italy, making her the only Italian city which, from her foundation until the arrival of Napoleon at the very end of the eighteenth century, was never once to be invaded or despoiled; secondly, they were to enable her to turn her back, as it were, on the peninsula and to direct her attention to the East – whence, through long centuries of successful commerce, her immense wealth was to come.

Thus, from the outset, the Venetians were conscious of being not as other men were, but a race apart. Whereas mainland Italians were landsmen, with a society founded on feudal tenure and an economy rooted in agriculture, they saw themselves as a merchant people of seafarers, for whom trade was not only the wellspring of their prosperity but also the basis of their entire social system. Without vast tracts of land to possess, there could be no feudalism of the kind that prevailed elsewhere; neither, therefore, could there be any aristocracy in the European sense of the word. In Venice and in Venice alone, the nobility was purely mercantile: trade was not demeaning, but an occupation of which to be proud.

And there was a difference, too, in cultural outlook. The rest of Italy sought its artistic and architectural inspiration in northern Europe and, to a rather lesser degree, in Rome; the Venetians, by contrast, looked east to Constantinople. In the early years of the lagoon settlements, such a tendency was not surprising: the neighbouring Byzantine exarchate, with its capital at Ravenna, exerted a considerable political influence on the embryo republic. But after the first quarter of the eighth century the exarchate came to an end; and Venice, if she had thought of herself as part of the *terra firma*, would doubtless have broken her links with Byzantium. That she did not do so demonstrated, more clearly than anything else could have done, the direction in which her inclinations lay.

It also did much to explain her architectural development, at least until the thirteenth century. The present Basilica of San Marco, for example – actually the third to occupy the site, and consecrated in 1094 – is in its essence a purely Byzantine conception, modelled (as were its two predecessors) on the imperial Church of the Holy Apostles at Constantinople. The same influence can be plainly seen in even earlier buildings, as for example the cathedral and its enchanting neighbour Santa Fosca on the island of Torcello, and the church of Santa Maria e San Donato on Murano; while back in the city we can still identify the remains of a number of splendid Byzantine *palazzi* – the most evocative of which is, for me, that great decorated round-headed arch in the north-west corner of the Corte Seconda del Milion (just behind the church of San Giovanni Crisostomo) which once formed part of the palace of Marco Polo himself.

In the field of decoration, Venice's Byzantine tradition continued even longer. The lovely fourteenth-century mosaics in the baptistery of San Marco, and those of the little chapel of San Isidore opposite it on the north side, murmur of Constantinople with every tessera; it was only in the 1520s that the rot began, when as a result of pressure by men who should have known better – Titian, Tintoretto and Veronese among them – quantities of exquisite medieval mosaics were removed and replaced by the abominations that we see today. (To

---

*opposite* Seen from the Doge's Palace, the island of San Giorgio Maggiore with its complex of monastic buildings.

The ornate, late fifteenth-century façade of the Scuola Grande di San Marco, recently cleaned by the Italian Government.

understand the full magnitude of the disaster, you have only to compare the glorious original mosaic above the extreme left-hand entrance on the west front with its four much later fellows in the corresponding lunettes to the right.) Another old eastern tradition was that of inlaying slabs of carved or coloured marble into the outside walls of buildings – that technique of 'incrustation' by which John Ruskin set so much store. So deeply rooted was this habit that, after lying dormant throughout the Gothic period, it reappeared with the Renaissance – in the work of the Lombardi, Mauro Coducci and their followers – to produce such magical effects as we see in the church of Santa Maria dei Miracoli or the little Palazzo Dario on the Grand Canal.

But if the Byzantine element in Venice's make-up was one of the first things that set her apart from her Italian fellow cities, there was another which conferred upon her a still more valuable distinction: her acquisition of the body of St Mark. Nowadays the importance of this event tends to be underestimated; in fact, it can hardly be overstressed. The point to remember is that Venice had no ancient history: she had not even existed in the great days of

The marble encrusted façade of the Palazzo Dario was added to an older Gothic structure in about 1487. The interior, many times rearranged and redecorated, was recently restored by its Venetian owner.

the Roman Empire. Consequently, in her first years as an independent republic, she was looked down on by the cities of the *terra firma* – and indeed by the rest of Europe – as a parvenu and an upstart. What she needed above all was prestige; and in those early Middle Ages, when religion and politics were still inextricably intertwined, the shortest cut to such prestige was to become the possessor of a really important relic. It was Venice's good fortune that according to an age-old legend the Evangelist, when travelling to Rome from his first diocese of Aquileia, had put in at the Rialtine islands – where the city now stands. There an angel had appeared to him, and had blessed him with those words, familiar to all Venetians, *'Pax tibi Marce, evangelista meus. Hic requiescet corpus tuum.'* (Peace unto you Mark, my evangelist. Here shall your body rest.) By a further stroke of luck, his body was known to have been buried in Alexandria – his last bishopric – beneath a tomb which had always been well-known in the city. It was therefore no particularly difficult task in 828 for two Venetian merchants to sail to Alexandria, bribe the custodians of the tomb, abstract the body, cover it in pork – the better to repel the attentions of the Muslim harbour guards – and return with it to Venice. There it was received with jubilation and laid to rest once again in a basilica especially prepared for it, immediately to the north of the Doge's Palace.

The Basilica of San Marco, however, was not the cathedral of Venice. Instead, by a typically Venetian decision, it was given the status of private chapel to the Doge, and was thus deliberately associated from the very beginning with the civil rather than the religious authorities of the state. Throughout the life of the Republic the seat of the Patriarch remained

---

No building in Venice better illustrates her Byzantine origins than the Basilica of San Marco, modelled on the Church of the Holy Apostles in Constantinople. The central doorway is under restoration.

*above* The lavish interior of the Basilica whose fabric and art treasures have been continuously maintained over the past seven hundred years by the Procuratoria di San Marco; *below* mosaics in the richly ornamented Zen Chapel which has only recently been reopened after restoration.

The cathedral church of Santa Maria and San Donato: chief glory of Murano and one of the greatest churches of Venice, it was among the few to be singled out for restoration under the Austrian Empire.

where it had always been – in the church of San Pietro di Castello, a building of relatively little architectural and still less ecclesiastical importance, tucked away in the extreme eastern corner of the city. Only in 1807 was it transferred to San Marco – but by then the Republic was ten years dead, the Basilica was a ducal chapel no longer, and Venice formed part of the Napoleonic Kingdom of Italy.

With the body of the Evangelist safely reinterred, Venice seemed to take on a new zest for life. The city's old protector, the dragon-slaying St Theodore, was forgotten – though his statue, for old time's sake, still stands (complete with distinctly improbable dragon) atop the western column in the Piazzetta – and St Mark's winged lion, painted on wood or canvas, carved in marble or stone, moulded in plaster or cast in bronze, but almost invariably bearing

A collection of St Mark's lions: *top left* a nineteenth-century copy of the *Leone molecca*, with the Gospel, inscribed in a circle; *top right* a lion-head keystone carved from Istrian marble; *below left* a leonine newel post in the fish market; *below right* a bronze lion perched on the early eighteenth-century gates of the Loggetta.

in its paw an open book upon which is inscribed the angel's pacific message, gradually became the ubiquitous emblem that it has remained to this day.

These, then, were the three all-important associations that moulded Venice in her

An unusual perspective on the Piazzetta, this early morning shot shows one of the ancient granite columns minus its incumbent – the winged lion has been taken down for restoration.

formative years: the sea, which afforded her the security that she needed – growing up as she did, not under the Pax Romana but in a period of anarchy and turbulence in which she could never otherwise have survived her infancy – and which permitted the development of the trade that made her great; Byzantium, which distanced her from the rest of Italy, giving a whole new dimension to her art and architecture and imbuing her with that instinct for sumptuousness and colour that permeates every aspect of her being; and St Mark himself – not just a shadowy patron but a real, continuing presence in Venetian life, through whom she acquired respect and reputation abroad and, among her own citizens, a consciousness of mystic privilege and protection.

And the tragedy of Venice is that, in each of these three associations, there was an ultimate betrayal.

First to be betrayed was Byzantium; and here the responsibility lay with the Republic itself. No lover of Venice likes to be reminded – still less to be obliged to remind others – of that blackest and most shameful chapter in Venetian history, ridiculously if ironically known as the Fourth Crusade; but the facts must be faced, and those facts are, very briefly, as follows.

The Third Crusade of 1189 had failed to recapture Jerusalem, lost to the Saracens two years before; and as the thirteenth century opened Pope Innocent III summoned Christendom to a renewed attempt. With the Turks now in virtual control of Anatolia the land route was no longer practicable, and negotiations were accordingly opened with Venice, the only Mediterranean power capable of transporting a vast crusading army by sea. The Republic agreed to make all the arrangements – for a fee – its reigning Doge (Enrico Dandolo, then at least seventy-five years old, perhaps considerably more, and almost stone-blind to boot) actually agreeing to lead a Venetian contingent himself; but when the Crusaders assembled on the Lido in June 1202 they found that they could not after all raise the sum required. They were therefore obliged, if they wished to leave at all, to accept Dandolo's terms: to stop on their way to the Holy Land at the former Venetian colony of Zara – now Zadar – then in Hungarian hands, and recapture it for Venice.

Zara lay only a short distance down the Adriatic, on the Dalmatian coast, and the army accomplished its task easily enough; while it was still there, however, it was sought out by the son of an exiled Byzantine emperor, promising immense rewards if it would now proceed to Constantinople, expel the usurping emperor and reinstate the exile on the throne. This too was done – Dandolo himself showing the utmost heroism by scrambling the first from his flagship as it was driven on to the beach. But now came disaster. The reinstated emperor found that he in his turn was unable to pay the Crusaders as he and his son had promised, while they for their part refused to leave with the debt unsettled. A second revolution followed; yet another emperor seized the throne; and the Crusaders – who had now by general, if tacit, agreement adopted Dandolo as their leader – seized Constantinople for themselves.

This time the carnage was dreadful; thousands were massacred, and when the killing was done the invaders fell on the city like locusts. The Frenchmen, Germans and Flemings who constituted the bulk of the army abandoned themselves to an orgy of destruction. The Venetians, by contrast, knew beauty when they saw it. They did not destroy; they simply looted, plundered and sent back to Venice everything of value that they could lay their hands on – beginning with the four great bronze horses which had dominated the Hippodrome since the days of Constantine and which thenceforth, for over seven centuries from their position on the west gallery of the Basilica, were similarly to dominate the Piazza San Marco. Finally, while a series of Frankish thugs set themselves up as emperors of Byzantium, old Dandolo presided over a division of the territorial spoils, acquiring for the Republic a three-eighths part of Constantinople and of all Byzantine dominions – and thereby laying, at a single stroke, the foundations of Venice's own formidable commercial empire.

Militarily, it had been a triumph; morally, it was indefensible. Although a Greek emperor was able to return to the city half a century later, and although his successors somehow managed to maintain themselves on the imperial throne for nearly two hundred years after that, Byzantium never recovered from the Fourth Crusade. Now permanently weakened and deprived of many of its richest and most strategically important possessions, it was incapable of any serious resistance to the ever-advancing Turks – who in their turn, on 29 May 1453, finally smashed their way into Constantinople. They have been there ever since.

Enrico Dandolo never returned to Venice. He died in Constantinople and was buried in St Sophia – where, in the gallery above the south aisle, his grave may still be seen. How strange, one feels, that there should be no memorial to him in his own city; for however calamitous the ultimate effects of the Fourth Crusade may have been in the wide context of world history, no

Doge ever did so much to increase the wealth, power and prosperity of Venice. On the other hand, few subsequent Doges had much opportunity to do so. Already in Dandolo's day that most astonishing of political phenomena, the Venetian constitution, was rapidly becoming crystallized; and before the thirteenth century was over it had taken the form that it was to preserve, essentially unchanged, for almost exactly five hundred years until the end came.

From its earliest beginnings it had been determinedly republican and democratic, with the Doge – the titular head of state – elected by the people for life. There was nothing especially remarkable about this; all the major north-Italian towns had adopted roughly similar arrangements. As time went on, however, more and more of these towns fell under the sway of some great family which gradually destroyed the local democratic institutions and established its own dictatorial power – the Visconti and the Sforza in Milan, the Gonzaga in Mantua, the Scaligeri in Verona, the Este in Ferrara. In Venice, too, certain of the early Doges had appointed a son as co-Doge in an attempt to make the position hereditary. But their subjects had, fortunately, reacted in time; and in the middle of the thirteenth century, in order to ensure that the supreme office of the Republic should never fall, directly or indirectly, into ambitious or unscrupulous hands, they devised what must be the most complicated system of election ever instituted by a civilized state.

---

The magnificent Gothic frontage of the Doge's Palace as seen from the campanile of San Giorgio Maggiore, with the mainland in the distance.

Looking across a hundred years from the quatrefoil tracery of the Doge's Palace loggia, completed in 1440, to Jacopo Sansovino's arcades for the Library of St Mark, begun in 1537 and described by Palladio as "the richest building built since classical antiquity".

On the day appointed for the election, the youngest member of the Signoria – the six-man inner council – was to pray in San Marco and then, on leaving, to stop the first boy he met and take him to the Doge's Palace, where all the members of the Great Council – the Maggior Consiglio – over the age of thirty were assembled. This boy, known as the *ballotino*, was to have the duty of picking the slips of paper from the urn during the drawing of lots. By the first of these lots, the Council chose thirty of their own number. The second reduced the thirty to nine, and these nine then voted for forty, each of whom had to have at least seven nominations. The forty would be reduced, again by lot, to twelve, whose task was to vote for twenty-five, of whom each required nine votes. These were again reduced to another nine; they voted for forty-five, who needed a minimum of seven votes each, and from whom the *ballotino* picked out eleven. These eleven now voted for forty-one – nine or more votes being required for each – and it was these to whom the actual ducal election was entrusted.

And all that was just the beginning. The electoral procedure itself, by which those forty-one finally picked the new Doge, was almost equally involved; but enough has been said to show the lengths to which the Venetians were prepared to go to ensure that their precious Dogeship should never, under any circumstances, be up for grabs.

Second to be betrayed was Venice's patron, St Mark. For over nine and a half centuries, from that day in 828 when they had carried his body in triumph into the basilica that they had prepared for it, the Venetians had accepted him and loved him as their own – more wholeheartedly, perhaps, than any other tutelary saint anywhere else on earth. Few cursory visitors to Milan or Florence – and still fewer to London or Paris – would be able to name the patron saints of those cities to save their lives; in Venice, on the other hand, it is hard indeed to spend ten minutes without encountering the evangelist in sign or symbol. As their guardian over the centuries he was to be worked hard and, on occasion, tried sorely; seldom, however, did he let them down. He presided over the growth of their commercial empire after the Fourth Crusade, his banner fluttering proudly over colonies and trading stations from the Baltic to the Black Sea and even beyond. In Venice itself, as the city steadily increased in splendour and opulence, his winged lion appeared in ever greater profusion, standing like a tremendous golden imprimatur on churches and *scuole*, hospitals and convents, educational institutions and government buildings.

Of all the winged lions of Venice, the grandest is that painted by Vittore Carpaccio now

---

The late fourteenth-century statues of Adam and Eve were placed on the corner of the Doge's Palace, with the Archangel brandishing his sword above, as an allegory of "The Severity of Good Government".

The heads of knights and crusaders were carved in the fourteenth century on one of the capitals of the ground floor arcade of the Doge's Palace, then replaced during the radical restoration begun in 1876.

hanging in the Doge's Palace. This magnificent beast is depicted in the act of stepping out of the water on to dry land, an act which effectively symbolizes the Republic's decision, early in the fifteenth century, to carve out for itself an empire on the Italian *terra firma*. Whether or not this step was well advised is a question that has been exhaustively debated over the years. In taking it, Venice was to a large extent transferring her attention away from the sea – an element which she knew and understood – to the land, with which she was relatively unfamiliar; she was also deliberately involving herself in Italian politics – something which in former times she had always been careful, whenever possible, to avoid. On the other hand, she knew that times were changing. Northern Italy was no longer essentially a bone of contention between Emperor and Pope (both of them usually absentees) as it had been in the Middle Ages; the towns themselves had now become the protagonists. As such they were growing stronger and more dangerous with every year that passed, and Venice could no longer afford the luxury of turning her back on them. Besides, her swelling population needed ever greater quantities of food. If there was territorial wealth to be gained on the mainland, she was determined to have her share.

Nor was this her only anxiety. By the middle of the fifteenth century, the Turks were beginning seriously to threaten her empire in the East. In the past hundred years the Ottoman armies had overrun more than half the Balkan peninsula – already by 1410 the

15

The campanile of San Giorgio Maggiore gives a superb panorama of the Giudecca Canal and Santa Maria della Salute – Baldassare Longhena's great seventeenth-century votive church.

be so lucky. And thus it has come about that the sea, for so long Venice's friend and protector, has now become her enemy – the final betrayal.

The 1966 flood, however, had one salutary result: it awoke the Italian government to the full magnitude of the danger that faced the most beautiful of its cities. Realizing that the problems were far too complex to be tackled by any single country and that disaster could be averted, if at all, only by an immense international effort, the government alerted UNESCO, and UNESCO in turn appealed to its member states; and the result has been a programme of conservation, restoration and rescue which, after twenty years, is still in progress: the most ambitious, most exciting project of its kind ever launched, aiming as it does to save not a building or group of buildings but a whole city – the most magical city in the world.

That programme, its successes and its achievements, is the subject of this book. The author, Peter Lauritzen, has lived in Venice for nineteen years and knows the city, every brick and stone of it, as well as anyone alive; while the photographers, Jorge Lewinski and Mayotte Magnus, have returned to it time and time again, at all seasons and in all weathers, and have documented the work that has been and is being done more thoroughly than ever before. Clearly, the result can be nothing more than an interim report; our task is not yet over. But it remains a complete and authoritative account, of a kind that has never previously been attempted, of an endeavour as unique, in its way, as Venice itself.

21

# INTRODUCTION

The author's opinions are, of course, his own. They do not invariably reflect those of the Venice in Peril Fund, nor is there any conceivable reason why they should. But they are not a jot the less valuable on that account, and I have been particularly happy to read what he has had to say about the admirable record of successive Italian governments in the story. For years now there has been a popular misconception, both in Europe and in America, that they have always refused to lift a finger for Venice, and have even allowed funds earmarked for the city to be misappropriated for other less worthy ends. Nothing, as the following pages make clear, could be further from the truth; and I can only hope that the ancient canard, now once again so firmly discredited, will at last be allowed to die. If future administrations, on the municipal, regional and national levels, are able to keep up the standards set by their predecessors; if the private organizations, Italian or foreign, continue to display the energy and determination that they have shown in the past; and if all individual lovers of the city, whether Venetian or not, are still prepared to make whatever contributions they can for its welfare; then I have no doubt in my mind that the great task will, in the fullness of time, be triumphantly completed and that Venice – a living, working Venice and not some sad, waterlogged museum – will survive for future centuries: a home for some, a dream for many, a joy and a lesson to us all.

John Julius Norwich

The Venice in Peril Fund
London, 1986

22

# Venice Submerged

THERE IS NOW A GENERATION of English-speaking students coming to Venice who were not born at the time of the 1966 floods. Yet much of what they know about Venice has been determined by that catastrophe and by contemporary accounts, both accurate and erroneous, of the events of that single dark November Saturday. There were two floods on 4 November: one which inundated Venice and another which swept through Florence with terrifying destructive force. They were quite separate phenomena and occurred for entirely different reasons. The consequences were just as different as the causes, yet both of these catastrophic floods drew attention to the plight of two of Europe's richest treasure houses of art and architecture.

It is seldom realized that the flood in Venice did not destroy, damage or even harm a single work of art, while in Florence the destruction was widespread and indeed a number of Florentines perished in the flooding. The Florence flood was caused by more than a month of heavy rainfall filling the Arno river reservoir full to overflowing. In order to avert a total catastrophe, the reservoir gates had to be opened, unleashing a flash flood on the unsuspecting city. The Venice flood was the result of a concatenation of freak coincidences: a south-east sirocco wind blowing at gale force during the winter equinox when the moon's gravitational pull acts with the greatest force on the upper Adriatic's swollen waters. The morning tide flowed into the Venetian lagoon, but the gale force winds prevented its ebb. The tide waters never receded. The afternoon's tidal flow virtually piled in upon the morning influx, creating a double tide of record proportions. For all its extraordinary configuration, this exceptional tide or *acqua alta*, as the Venetians call it, rose slowly, indeed inexorably in the normal fashion. It was none the less alarming for all that. It soon reached the height of the city's fuel oil storage tanks, recently filled for the winter season's central heating. The tanks burst, coating the rising waters with a layer of black petroleum pollution. Electricity failed and, as dusk fell, the city was plunged in darkness, relieved here and there with the faint glow of candlelight.

Just before nightfall, at about five in the afternoon, the steady rise of the lagoon level was

Sea water swirling over one of the lowest points in the city, the waterfront arcades of the Doge's Palace, during an *acqua alta*, Venice's high water. *(Ermanno Reberschak)*

given a great jolt. The combination of an earth tremor on the Adriatic sea bed and a seiche, or false tidal wave, whipped the seas into a frenzy of force that crashed through the ancient Murazzi sea walls on the Lido. The outer islands suffered this added affliction first and took the full force of the watery assault. Hundreds of acres of market gardens and cultivated fields were submerged. The force of the storm tore heavy fishing trawlers from their moorings and stripped the Lido beaches of cabanas and bathing cabins. The damage was immense. But it was the outer islands that had borne the brunt and, apart from the gusting gales of sirocco wind felt in the city, the battering force of the sea was dissipated by the time it reached the heart of Venice.

Nonetheless, the *acqua alta* had reached a record height of over six feet as measured in the Piazza San Marco, the lowest point in the city. The thought of flood waters lying over six feet deep in the world's most famous and beautiful square conjures a catastrophic vision. And that was the picture that the foreign press presented to an astonished world as soon as communications with the city returned to normal. For the Venetians, the reality was somewhat different: the city's tidal flux is always measured from the mean sea level, some

---

The storms that produced the freak double tide of 4 November 1966 drove the waters up to a record height in the Piazza San Marco.

twenty-seven and a half inches below the city's pavement, so the water in the Piazza actually lay some four feet deep at its deepest. The height above sea level also varies considerably within the 117 islands that make up Venice, not to mention the variations on each individual island. The Rialto, for example, takes its name from the fact that its island has a particularly high bank or *rivo alto* while an entire section of the city, the *sestiere* of Dorsoduro is called the hard-backed quarter from the height and firmness of its soil. Indeed there were parts of Venice that were not covered at all by the flooding on 4 November but nonetheless the flood did render normal traffic and communication within the city impossible. Nothing could pass under the low bridges spanning the hundreds of small, swollen, side canals and even though the public water buses or *vaporetti* continued to circulate in the Grand Canal, they could not risk crossing to the Lido after the Murazzi had broken. Walking around most quarters of the flooded city was only possible wearing the wading boots that many Venetians keep on hand for work among the stake net fish traps of the lagoon shoals, yet the railway station and car park islands were high and dry, as were the rail and road causeways that link Venice to the mainland. Eventually the flood waters receded and by nine o'clock that night, the Venetians could walk about dryshod to inspect the damage. They found rubbish and detritus scattered everywhere and a slimy coating of black fuel oil stained walls and pavements, although much had floated out to sea on the ebb. Electricity was still out of order and the waters had ruined central heating units installed in ground-floor rooms. But no one had died in the flood and no work of art was damaged.

The story of the flood in Florence was quite different, yet it bears recounting because ultimately it was the damage done in Florence that changed the entire history of Venice in the twentieth century. By the evening of 3 November, forty days of incessant rainfall had filled an up-stream reservoir on the Arno river to danger point. The official in charge of the reservoir was off duty that night and the custodian was faced with the choice of consulting a manual of instructions or ringing through to Rome to wake the Minister of the Interior. He chose the former course and learned that once the danger point was reached, as it would inevitably be on Saturday 4 November, he must open the gates of the reservoir. If not, the accumulated weight of water would break down the gates and send a flood of water through Florence capable of destroying virtually everything in its path. As it was, the flood that he unleashed on the sleeping city was unlike anything in living memory. The Arno had overflowed its banks from time to time, but this was a flash flood of terrifying force. The swollen river quickly spilled over the tall retaining walls and poured down the sloping embankments into the lower sections of the city. It pushed, floated and even overturned heavy automobiles, finally hurling them through fences, gates and into lampposts. Cellars filled quickly and heavy black fuel oil was carried out into the streets on the surface of the swirling, raging current. Water poured into the underpass by the Santa Maria Novella railway station, trapping and drowning dozens of people. Fortunately that Saturday was a national holiday in Italy and so there were fewer Florentines on the streets than usual and no schoolchildren at all. Many of the city's poor abandoned their ground-floor rooms for safety above, but others were too old or infirm to move and simply stayed where they were, not believing that the waters could rise any further. The threat seemed remote in districts that lay fully a half mile from the river but as the day progressed, the Florentines realized that virtually no one would be spared. Heating, electricity and water supplies all failed and would not return to normal for some three weeks after the waters had receded.

The city was also effectively cut off from the outside world as landslides in the surrounding hills downed telephone lines. Once communication was re-established, the world learned of the tragic toll the flood had taken in Florence. The Florentines themselves were profoundly shocked by the number of people killed by the flood waters though grateful that many had been spared by the providential holiday. Next, they were simply shattered by the scale of the destruction. While a wartime air-raid might have left large parts of a city unscathed, here nothing had escaped damage. The Florentines were never to forget the tourists and curiosity seekers who swarmed into the city avid for sensation – 'jackals' they were called – nor did they forgive the government for being so very slow in coming to the aid of the stricken city. The Mayor of Florence convoked the first town council meeting in his own house in the devastated Santa Croce district so they would see for themselves the extent of the destruction. Many of the Councillors had come completely unprepared and had to be borne to the meeting on the backs of the Mayor's neighbours. The flood waters had risen over twenty feet in the cloister of the great Franciscan church nearby and braces had to be erected across the narrow streets to prevent the collapse of entire palace façades undermined by the force of the waters. When the President of the Republic finally deigned to visit Florence, he was spat upon by the outraged populace; still the government did little or nothing.

Florence and the Florentines were fighting what seemed a battle for survival. Food supplies had to be delivered in special rail convoys and were distributed from sidings in the Florence railway station. There was no drinking water in the city nor even any water that could be used for washing or cleaning: indeed, one of the earliest and most useful gestures from abroad was a gift from Holland – an amazing machine that could convert drain water into water pure enough for drinking. The British Consul in Florence immediately contacted the organizers of a recent British Week trade fair and hundreds of kerosene stoves began to arrive from Scotland. Fortunately the rain stopped on 5 November and the weather, for late autumn in Tuscany, turned quite mild. Still the stoves and the water purifier were received with gratitude.

Later on this early assistance tended to be overshadowed by the publicity given to the students who flocked to Florence to help dry out books and manuscripts damaged in the flooding of the Biblioteca Nazionale cellars, although these well-meaning young people were never quite so warmly received by the average Florentine as the foreign press led the world to believe. Their presence in the city simply put an additional strain on scarce provisions and housing; in fact, many of them had to be lodged in sleeping carriages in the railway station.

The truth is that the Florentines alone were responsible for their city's recovery – a fact worth emphasizing, especially in the light of all the subsequent self-congratulation generated abroad over the rescue of Florentine works of art. The Florentines were much more impressed by the offer of the Fiat motor car company to replace any flood-damaged car with a new Fiat at half-price. Of course, local garages made it possible for anyone to have his car 'flooded' for a nominal fee and the automobile population of Florence doubled overnight! The city was functioning normally again just in time for Pope Paul VI's galvanizing and unprecedented personal visit on Christmas Eve – an event now forgotten by all, save the Florentines who were there at the time.

In the meantime, reports of the two floods had raised a widespread alarm outside Italy. Florence and Venice, treasure houses of Europe's cultural heritage, had suffered a catastrophe of gigantic proportions, and details of the damaged works of art began to assume prominence in the foreign press as other aspects of the floods receded into comparative insignificance. The fact that two such cities had been struck on the same day far overshadowed the fact that no work of art had been damaged in Venice and that in Florence, the inhabitants were more concerned with day-to-day survival than with the city's art treasures. Not all the early reports were clear in their sense of the priorities involved.

The official French emissary reported that little or no permanent harm had been done to works of art in Florence but there was no such cavalier attitude in press releases issued to the English-speaking world. The British immediately organized an International Art and Archives Rescue Fund while the Americans formed an even more dramatically styled Committee to Rescue Italian Art. For both these fund-raising groups the emphasis was on rescue and not, as yet, on restoration. Cimabue's great Crucifix, torn from the refectory wall at Santa Croce and later found lying deep in the oil-soaked mud, became the symbol of the entire international rescue campaign, and an excellent illustration of the way in which scientific restoration techniques can be used to recreate something of the dramatic impact of a damaged masterpiece. But apart from the spectacular and, as it turned out, virtually irreparable loss of the great medieval crucifix, the worst damage appeared to have been suffered by the documents and papers of the State Archives, stored in the Biblioteca Nazionale overlooking the Arno. However, like the treasures of the Pitti and Uffizi Galleries, the most precious archival material had always been housed well above ground. The flooding had done its worst in the cellars which contained mostly printed books and secondary source material. The funds collected abroad for the rescue of these archives paid unexpected dividends: hundreds upon thousands of books were salvaged. They were washed of the mud that had turned them into solid clay blocks, their pages were painstakingly separated from one another, cleaned of stains and hung up to dry. It was then that astonishing treasures began to come to light: pages of ancient illuminated texts that had been inadvertently bound with later printed books, incunabula and autograph parchments of rare value. Such was the trove that lay revealed that the restorers could mount an exhibition entirely devoted to the newly discovered works of art.

In the course of this rescue operation a great deal was learned about the restoration of leather, paper, parchment and books in general. New techniques were developed and the most successful taught to the eager apprentices that had materialized in Florence from every corner of Europe and America. The emergence of these new techniques and methods in the course of a rescue operation prefigured much of what has happened in Venice in the two decades since the flood of 4 November 1966. But for the first year, 1966-7, when funds were being gathered abroad to aid the rescue operation, the world's attention was clearly focused on Florence and Venice benefited only tangentially. After all, these monies were being collected to rescue works of art, and Florence clearly had the greater and more urgent need.

After the Cimabue Crucifix and the flooded archives of the Biblioteca Nazionale came Florence's immense patrimony of mural painting executed in the fresco technique. This rescue work was far more painstaking and consequently received less publicity at first. Refectories, chapels and churches where frescos had been damaged by the flood waters were simply closed to the public for years at a time while highly qualified experts – for the most part Italian technicians with the occasional help of foreign advisers – worked together with professionally trained and highly skilled restoration teams. There was no room for amateur volunteers and the work was scheduled to last as long as it took to rescue and restore the damaged frescos. The fresco technique of mural painting is perhaps the most distinctive and characteristic contribution of Florence and, by extension, Tuscany to European art. From Giotto through the Sienese and Florentine masters of the Gothic fourteenth century to the Renaissance painters active in the fifteenth century – Masaccio, Fra Angelico, Piero della Francesca, Benozzo Gozzoli, Verrochio, Ghirlandaio, Botticelli and Leonardo – culminating in the heirs of the great Tuscan tradition working in Rome, Raphael and Michelangelo, fresco painting is a Florentine art form. Because of Venice's climate, it plays virtually no part at all in Venetian art yet Venice profited immeasurably from the lessons learnt in the restoration of the frescos in Florence.

These lessons were of a brutal simplicity. The danger to frescos from rising damp was multiplied a millionfold as flood waters swirled around the base and soaked into the very fabric of masterpieces by Paolo Uccello in the Green Cloisters at Santa Maria Novella (subsequently closed to the public for almost fifteen years), Andrea Castagno at Sant'Apollonia or Andrea del Sarto, whose cycle in the atrium of Santissima Annunziata is still under restoration. The paintings themselves and their colours proved remarkably resistant, but the walls on which the final wet (*fresco*) ground of plaster was laid frequently threatened to come away from their lattice-work supports. This was a matter of structural repair rather than cosmetic restoration, yet it was just such problems that would arise most often in Venice. The Florentine frescos had to be removed from their damp-soaked walls. The walls were then dried out and insulated before the cleaned and restored frescos were returned to their original positions.

The fuel oil that had floated on the surface of the rising flood waters, leaving a black stain on the wall surface after the waters receded, represented an even greater threat to Florentine works of art. Again fresco proved a remarkably resilient medium and after careful chemical analysis, solvents were concocted that would clean away the oil stains without causing harm to the colours of the painting. As early as 1969 a number of salvaged and restored examples joined an exhibition in London, entitled 'Frescos from Florence'.

Precisely one year after the flood, in early November 1967, there occurred an event that was to alter the pattern of rescue work in Italy, turning the entire world's attention from Florence to Venice and consequently bringing to a close an era of Venetian history that began with the destruction of the Most Serene Republic in 1797. On 3 November 1967 Venice was the victim of another exceptionally high *acqua alta*. This time the sirocco, Venice's prevailing south-easterly wind, was not blowing at gale force, nor was there a seiche, nor an earthquake on the bottom of the Adriatic, but nonetheless the tide rose to within eight inches of the extraordinary 1966 flooding. Water stood just over three feet deep in the Piazza San Marco and photographs of the 1967 *acqua alta* received almost as much international publicity as the infinitely more dramatic episode the previous year. The foreign press and the mass communications media led the world to believe that this flooding had become a permanent condition of life in Venice. The American television networks were so convinced by their own perception of Venetian life that in early November 1968, the National Broadcasting Company and the Columbia Broadcasting System sent television crews to cover the annual event. Unfortunately for them, there was no high water that November, nor did the phenomenon repeat itself in any sensational or even significant form in the three succeeding years.

In 1972 the *acqua alta* was back again, although not in any abnormal fashion. But the absence of flooding, supposedly good news for the Venetians, would not sell newspapers abroad and what was not generally realized was that the majority of Venetians are, and always have been, quite resigned to the *acqua alta*. It is part of the life of their city, much as other cities might experience exceptionally heavy snowfall, rendering city services inoperative and possibly causing the schools to close. Such a comparison is of limited value, however, because Venetian schools are not closed during the average *acqua alta*. The children may have to wear rubber boots to get to their classes, but by the time they come home for lunch, the streets will be dry. Even during the worst *acqua alta* Venice's water-bound public transport will continue to function and shopkeepers, whose shelves and stocks are always positioned well above flood level, can usually repair high-water 'damage' to their shops with some sawdust and a broom. Venice's *acqua alta*, even that of 1966, should never be compared with a blizzard elsewhere or the flood in Florence. No one died in Venice's 1966 *acqua alta*, nor was any damage done to a single work of art.

What then raised the alarm? Why, since then, have people everywhere been convinced of the need to preserve Venice? At first it was undeniably the threat of repeated flooding, even though the phenomenon itself was neither completely nor accurately understood. In the year between the two floods, statisticians began to take a closer look at the Venetian condition. Charts demonstrated that high-water flooding seemed to be more frequent in recent decades than in the past and that, by 1967, the severity of the flooding was following a geometrical progression. From our current vantage point, twenty years on, we know that this interpretation of the available statistics was not wholly accurate.

In addition to the predicted increased frequency of flooding in Venice, the vexed question of subsidence contributed to the general alarm over the condition of the city. Ever since the first solidly constructed building replaced wooden housing in the eleventh or twelfth century, Venice has been slowly subsiding into its mud-flat foundations. The rate of this sinking was always something of an enigma until statisticians made some alarming calculations that foretold disaster. Once again, we now know that these dire predictions were quite misleading.

In both cases, the only reasonably accurate data available for the flooding and the subsidence was very recent – no more than a hundred years old in the case of the *acqua alta* – and scientists now admit that only data of the last forty years can satisfy their criteria of accuracy. Yet even more fundamental to the Venetian problem and its analysis is the reluctance of scientists and statisticians to acknowledge the frequently demonstrated fact that Venice is unpredictable. The same scientists who were once completely dedicated to the theory of Venice's progressive subsidence have now put forward the claim that the city has not only stopped sinking, but that in the twelve month period from 1984-5, it has risen by a full two centimetres!

But the scientists and statisticians who had examined the Venetian condition between 1966 and 1967 drew their own conclusions and broadcast them to the world. Thanks to the dramatic *acqua alta* of 3 November 1967, the cry was taken up by the world at large and dire predictions abounded in the foreign press. These predictions continued to be fashionable for many years with surprising consequences for the city. Only a few commented on the slight absurdity of it all and recalled the memoirs of English delegates at the Congress of Vienna who had written in 1814 that Venice would not last another fifty years. Today the jeremiads of 1967 seem almost as absurd as those of 1814.

Hysteria characterized a great deal written about Venice in the foreign press in the decades following the flood of 1966, but it was just this high-flown, melodramatic publicity that reversed the slow and seemingly inexorable decline and deterioration of the city and brought about her preservation. Venice Preserved indeed, but which Venice? The apparently frequent flooding and the gradual subsidence seemed to indicate that Venice was slipping into a watery grave or at least that the city might become completely uninhabitable in the foreseeable future. The alarm raised over these aspects of the Venetian problem meant that the world at large became concerned with the preservation of Venice as a city to live in. The world would help preserve the Venice of the Venetians.

Anyone who has kept abreast of developments in Venice in the last few years will realize that things have turned out very differently. The Venice of the Venetians has been of much less interest than the Venice of Art and Culture which – it has even been argued – does not belong to the Venetians at all, but rather to the world. The reason for this disastrously distorted approach can be sought in those first years after the floods of 1966 and 1967. The world had gathered funds to rescue and restore the arts and the archives of Florence and those of Venice, too. Following the onslaught of the second exceptional *acqua alta*, the international administrators of these funds began to examine more carefully the condition of works of art and monuments in Venice. Their discoveries appalled them and gave rise to the mammoth, and largely successful, campaign to preserve Venetian art.

There had already been efforts made to restore works of art in Venice, but in the light of subsequent developments – and especially given the scale of later international fund-raising for restoration work in Venice – these early initiatives were virtually forgotten, a particular shame as it encouraged the further misconception that the Venetians had never done anything to preserve the monuments of their beautiful city. The story of one of these early projects, carried out in the 1950s and today still considered the largest and most impressive restoration programme ever privately undertaken by a single Venetian, belongs to a later stage in this narrative.

A full five years before the 1966 flood in Venice, the Fondazione Ercole Varzi financed the restoration of all the painted decoration in the small, remote church of San Sebastiano. This church, once part of a wealthy monastic foundation, now survives as a shrine to one of the great artistic geniuses of Venice's Golden Century. Paolo Cagliari, universally known as Veronese, first decorated the church's sacristy with ceiling canvases in 1555. By the time of his death and burial in San Sebastiano some thirty-three years later, he had enriched virtually every surface of the handsome building with the glowing colours and dazzling perspectives of his grand vision. St Sebastian's popularity as a protector against the Plague supported this wealth of decoration in the sixteenth century, but after Napoleon closed and suppressed Venice's monasteries, San Sebastiano fell on hard times and Veronese's wonderful cycle of paintings succumbed to the ravages of time and neglect. The Fondazione Ercole Varzi's contributions made it possible for the Italian government's two Superintendents to restore both the paintings and the building, and the work was nearing completion when the freak *acqua alta* of 4 November 1966 struck Venice. The rising waters weakened the foundations of one of the church's walls to the extent that wooden buttresses had to be constructed to prevent its collapse. This perilous state of affairs attracted some of the first financial assistance provided in Venice by the American Committee to Rescue Italian Art.

A great deal of early restoration in Venice was basically structural work. There were

leaking roofs, unsound walls riddled with rising damp, and flooring that concealed foundations constantly undermined and eroded by the rise and fall of excessive tides. While major monuments and important buildings such as historic churches attracted the most attention at first, there had already been a vanguard action in the year before the flood when Venice's Italia Nostra financed the restoration of a row of minor houses in the city's Dorsoduro quarter. The Venice section of this national group dedicated to the preservation of Italy's artistic and environmental heritage had been established in 1958 and the following year published a pamphlet, *Italia Nostra Difende Venezia*, which can still be used as a guide to the issues fundamental to any campaign to preserve Venice.

Thus even before the flood of 1966, there existed the beginnings of a dichotomy that is entrenched in the structure of local and national administrations and divides Venice down to the present day. Initially, there was no clear separation or schism between the Venice of the monuments and the Venice of the Venetians – the city to be looked at and the city to be lived in. It was the funds collected abroad after the 1966 *acqua alta* that fomented the dichotomy because these monies were applied almost exclusively to the repair and restoration of works of art and monuments. And yet the alarm had been sounded over Venice's survival as a city in which to live, a city safe from flooding and sinking. The reason for this volte-face lies in the fact that preventing the rise of the *acqua alta* simply proved beyond anybody's capabilities (and still represents a dilemma for the most serious students of the problem), while the city's sinking seemed to be part of a millennial process that it would be quite impossible to reverse. And in addition to these principal considerations, restoration of the buildings that the Venetians actually lived in was extremely complicated, if not impossible. There existed no mechanism for the Italian government, let alone foreign benefaction, to contribute to the repair or restoration of private property.

As the foreign committees dedicated to the preservation of Venice increasingly devoted their energies to works of art and monuments, there emerged one international organization which tried to focus the attention of the world and of the Italian authorities on the problem as a whole. Less than a month after the first terrible floods, the Director General of the United Nations Educational, Scientific and Cultural Organization appealed to all mankind on behalf of both Florence and Venice. Today UNESCO may be widely discredited in the English-speaking world, but at the time of the floods and in the twenty years since, it has played an important, if frequently misinterpreted, role in the campaign to preserve Venice. In 1967 UNESCO set up an office in Rome to co-ordinate its initiatives and activities on behalf of Florence and Venice with those of the Italian authorities. Later, as the complexity and scale of Venice's problems became more evident, the office was moved from Rome to Venice itself. In striking contrast to the accusations of extravagant over-staffing and financial waste directed at the parent organization and its Paris headquarters, the Venice branch has always seemed something of a shoestring affair. At first the staff consisted of three people: a director, his assistant and a single secretary. Later this was further reduced with the departure of the director, leaving the entire operation in the capable hands of one of the most outstanding

---

*opposite* The sixteenth-century church of San Sebastiano enshrines masterpieces from every phase of Paolo Veronese's career. The paintings, frescos and altarpieces were all restored 1961-64 by the Ercole Varzi Foundation.

personalities in the entire international campaign to see Venice preserved, Baronessa Maria Teresa Rubin. She has been the inspiration behind a number of initiatives, described elsewhere, that have changed the very nature of contemporary Venice, but her principal task has been to co-ordinate most of the world's donations for and interest in the preservation of the city and its treasures. In this she has been perfectly faithful to UNESCO's original intentions. Despite the widespread misconception, UNESCO does not finance projects, neither does it organize them. It will employ staff, largely locally recruited, to organize the analysis of a problem, calling on expert opinion from all over the world. It will further organize research, discussion groups and scholarly symposia and then publish a report, sometimes incorporating solutions recommended by the participating experts. If its analysis and report are accepted as useful to the government concerned, and if that government finds the solutions too costly to implement, then UNESCO may call on its constituent members – potentially all the member countries of the United Nations – to assist the country in question. This aid may take the form of expert advice, technical assistance, scientific equipment or even international loans negotiated under especially favourable terms.

This was the pattern of UNESCO's participation in the well-known project to rescue the temples of Abu Simbal in Egypt. However, the problems encountered there were of a far simpler order than anything in Venice: an analysis of what needed to be done at Abu Simbal was prepared, expert recommendations were made and the whole was submitted to the Egyptian government. The problem, though immense, was solved with admirable alacrity. To compare this situation with the preservation of Venice may seem a sterile exercise, but it does help emphasize the bureaucratic complexities that were encountered in Venice: every solution offered – whether by UNESCO itself or by the proliferating international committees and their consultant experts, or by critics and historians in general – had to be submitted for the approval first of the local government of the municipality of Venice, then the government of the Province, the government of the Veneto Region, and finally the national government of the Italian Republic. Each of these different levels of government reflects an entirely different political complexion as Italy's twenty-odd political parties will be represented in different, and often conflicting, proportions. To complicate matters further, since the foundation of the Italian Republic forty years ago the national government has changed, on average, every eight months and with each of these changes of government new ministers will assume office. They will then introduce new policies according to their own political persuasions which may well be quite different from those of the Prime Minister. In a political system such as this – once described as the most sophisticated in the world – the potential for negotiation and legislative revision is infinite.

In fact none of these government offices received any concrete proposals on behalf of Venice for some time. Meanwhile the UNESCO office in Rome made two important contributions to the future pattern of restoration work. The first reflected the increasing concern with the state of works of art and monuments in Venice, even though not a single work of art had been damaged either by the 1966 flood or the *acqua alta* of 1967. Towards the end of 1967, the UNESCO office, in conjunction with the Superintendent of Galleries, recruited seven work teams to compile a card index cataloguing the state of preservation of painting, sculptures and the few frescos in the city. By the following year, there were over sixteen thousand cards in existence. On the initiative of the International Council of Monuments and Sites, UNESCO then promoted the compilation of a second card index, this time in collaboration with the Italian government's Superintendency of Monuments in Venice. This catalogue, detailing the condition of some four hundred palaces, a hundred or so churches, thirty convents and twenty Venetian *scuole*, was completed in early 1969.

In the same year, UNESCO published its *Rapporto su Venezia*. In the opening words of his preface, the Director General declared, 'We must save Venice: we must and we can do it.' It was a splendid assertion and represented a commitment that has been well-honoured. However, the remainder of the preface was composed largely of questions. And quite rightly, too: even today we do not have all the answers. The bulk of the report was an admirable compilation of graphs and statistics concentrating first on the problems of the lagoon, subsidence and the environment. The second section dealt with the demography of the Venetian population, while the section concerning the artistic, monumental and cultural heritage of the city came last in spite of the Director General's prediction that this represented the only part of the problem likely to attract immediate attention and action. In this he proved completely correct. The UNESCO report has been all too little known in the English-speaking world: indeed the first, and for years the only, edition was published in Italian. Ostensibly and sensibly, it was addressed to the Italian authorities.

The UNESCO report did not reach the public at large, but then neither was the English-speaking world quite ready for it. A series of accidents in the history of taste and fashion had led to the virtual neglect of Venice and the story of Venetian art and culture in the first half of the twentieth century. This can perhaps best be illustrated by the fact that in 1971, when Sir Kenneth Clark was preparing his impressive television series 'Civilization', he omitted any mention of Venice. But what was even more revealing was that hardly anyone noticed his oversight then, while today – when Venice has become so popular – they can hardly believe it. At the time, the English-speaking world had become accustomed to hearing about Florence and the achievements of the Florentine Renaissance whenever the subject of Italian art and culture was broached. And the history of the Venetian Republic, which had never contributed much to the mainstream of European history, had suffered from a similar neglect in the English-speaking world. In 1971 the only history of Venice in English was the historical sketch of the Republic written by Horatio Brown in 1895.

If the UNESCO report were republished today in English, it would probably prove a best seller as does much of what is written about Venice now. But it was not the UNESCO report that opened the world's eyes to Venice's environmental problems. Initially public interest was focused almost solely on the preservation of the city's artistic treasures and it is only now, twenty years after the *acqua alta* of 1966, that consideration is being given to the problems of the lagoon, Venice's geographical situation and the Venetian population which the report rightly put at the top of its list of priorities. UNESCO certainly helped the Italian authorities determine the needs of the arts by compiling the two extensive card indexes mentioned above. But if the 1966 flood did no damage to works of art in Venice, why were the city's art treasures found to be in such perilous condition – far worse, in fact, than those in flood-ravaged Florence?

The simple answer is that Venice, its art and its monuments had suffered too long from poverty, abandonment and neglect. The 1967 *acqua alta* could be said to have marked the one hundred and seventieth anniversary of the death of Venice. And only now, twenty years after that nadir in Venice's fortunes, is the city coming to life again. It is an extraordinary story and bears repeating, at least in its outline.

# Dying Venice

THE GLORY OF VENICE CAME INTO EXISTENCE because of the Serenissima Repubblica, the political organization through which the Venetian islanders transformed their settlement in an inhospitable environment into the richest city in the world. The 117 mud-flat islands became a metropolis of two hundred thousand inhabitants at a time when medieval Paris had a population of forty thousand, London was inhabited by twenty thousand and Rome a mere fifteen thousand. It developed into a city of legendary artistic riches. Even today the number of treasures preserved in situ in Venice is dazzling although recent estimates suggest that only four per cent of the original horde survives intact, the rest having been dispersed in the nineteenth century. Alvise Zorzi's magisterial catalogue of vanished Venice, *Venezia Scomparsa*, traces the tragic tale of the dispersal through two full, melancholy volumes.

Venice's moveable treasures began to disappear shortly after the destruction of the Venetian Republic in 1797. Only two weeks before his final declaration of war against Venice, the twenty-six-year-old general of the French Revolutionary Army in Italy, Napoleon Bonaparte, reverted to the Italian of his ancestors to pronounce the death sentence on the Republic: *'Io non voglio più Senato, non voglio più inquisitori: io sarò un Atilla per lo Stato Veneto!'* 'I will have no more Senate; I will not have Inquisitors: I shall be an Atilla for the Venetian State!' Between the first eight-month occupation of Venice by the armies of the French Revolution in 1797 and the end of the French emperor's Regno Italico some seventeen years later, Napoleon proved true to his terrible words. His agents not only ransacked the treasury of San Marco, prising loose gemstones from their ancient settings, but they catalogued more than twelve thousand paintings suitable for confiscation from the monasteries, convents, churches and *scuole* suppressed under the Napoleonic regime. Suppressions and confiscations were, of course, the time-honoured way of financing a military campaign. General Bonaparte also collected a personal store of booty with which to impress the people of Paris and launch himself on a political career, the ambition of which is still astonishing.

# DYING VENICE

The riches of the Louvre and the Brera Gallery display Napoleon's excellent taste in loot to this day. Venice, however, fared sadly with the mutilation of all St Mark's winged lions, the scuttling of the Venetian fleet, the dismemberment and burning of the *Bucintoro*, the great golden barge of state with which the Doge went annually to espouse the sea, and the complete despoliation of the Doge's Palace. It was a barbaric sack of methodical thoroughness.

But all of this was nothing compared with the death blow Napoleon dealt Venice itself. By dismantling the millennial constitution and abolishing all Venice's ancient institutions, he deprived the entire patriciate, Venice's governing class, of its very *raison d'être*. Serious historians have gone so far as to toy with theories of racial suicide in describing what happened when one third of Venice's patrician families died out in the first generation after Napoleon's annihilation of the Republic. The ancient and distinguished Contarini family provides a remarkable illustration of this phenomenon. In 1797 it had seventeen active branches and had given the Republic more Doges than any other. But in 1836, with the death of Count Giacomo Contarini, Chamberlain of the Austrian Empire, there disappeared the very last member of this once numerous and flourishing clan.

Economic historians have often insisted that the Venetian Republic had been living on borrowed time, if not borrowed capital, long before Napoleon's advent. Many have sought the turning point in Venice's fortunes in the fall of Constantinople to the Turks in 1453; others point to the Venetians' own alarm over the Portuguese circumnavigation of Africa; still others indicate the loss of Crete or the surrender of the Peloponnese after Francesco Morosini's short-lived re-conquest. All agree, however, that the eighteenth century, for all its outward show of wealth and apparent prosperity, was an epoch of economic and moral decay and decline. This is not the place to quibble with generalizations based on hindsight. There can be no doubt that Venice's maritime economy was seriously weakened in the late eighteenth century. Whatever the Republic's recuperative powers may have been, Napoleon never gave them a chance. Besides systematically scuttling her fleet and sacking the great Arsenal shipyards, thus destroying the livelihood of thousands of working-class Venetians, he abolished the framework and structure that supported not only the patriciate, but also the citizen middle classes from whom the Republic's chancery officials and administrative bureaucrats were recruited. He also suppressed Venice's *scuole*, the charitable confraternities of the middle classes, whose wealth had endowed hospitals, hospices, orphanages and provided free housing for the poor. Like many other victorious generals before him, Napoleon closed innumerable monastic foundations in order to seize their riches. Artistic treasures such as Paolo Veronese's immense masterpiece, 'The Miracle at Cana', were sent, along with hundreds of other paintings, to Paris where they still hang in the Louvre, while monastery assets were used to finance further campaigning. Besides providing Napoleon with much needed capital, these suppressions and confiscations destroyed a centuries-old economy. The monasteries had always been essential to economic life in Europe. They employed thousands of peasant workers and other dependents who suddenly found themselves cut adrift as ·revolutionary fervour worked out its irrational rage on small communities of religious brethren, insignificant in themselves, but in the eyes of the Revolution, custodians of centuries of accumulated wealth.

This short account serves to illustrate why Venice's churches, and particularly her monastic establishments, were unable to support themselves through the decades that followed the Napoleonic conquest of the Republic. It also explains how Venice's Accademia Gallery, founded by Napoleon's stepson, Eugène de Beauharnais (styled *Son Altesse Imperial, le Prince de Venise* [*sic*]), came to be so extremely rich in paintings of the Venetian school. The Accademia had been created as the principal repository for art treasures removed from suppressed monasteries and *scuole* after the distribution of the best pieces to the Louvre in Paris and the Brera Gallery in Milan, Napoleon's vice-regal capital. Beauharnais deserves great credit for the creation of the gallery, but his stepfather also merits an honourable mention for his policy of collecting works of art rather than destroying them as had been the custom during the Revolution in France itself, the Iconoclastic Fury in sixteenth-century Flanders and the Reformation in England. Napoleon's *coup de grâce* was not dealt to the world of Venetian art, but to the Venice of the Venetians. Yet at first, he did not occupy Venetian territories long enough to understand the scope of the blow that he had dealt the Republic. In revolutionary France, an entrepreneurial middle class had risen to power partly financed by the redistributed wealth of the monastic orders. In Venice this wealth went to pay foreign armies while monastic holdings, along with all the Republic's remaining territories, were sold, within eight months, into the hands of another occupying power.

The Austrian armies of the Holy Roman Empire entered Venice in mid-January 1798, initiating a military occupation that was to last, save for the brief interval of Napoleon's return to Venice as Emperor of the French, for more than half of the nineteenth century. While the *ancien régime* style of the Austrians may at first have seemed more congenial than the brief but brutal occupation of a self-styled Attila, Venice suffered just the same. According to the liberal historian, G.M. Trevelyan, the Austrians treated the Venetians with greater fairness and justice than was enjoyed by contemporary Englishmen under the tyranny of the Justices of the Peace and the Rotten Borough system. However, the imperial government manifested no interest in Venice or in the fate of the Venetians whatsoever. Austria favoured Trieste as its principal seaport and naval base and Venice began its long career as a victim of neglect. By 1817 it was estimated that one quarter of the city's population, fully fifty thousand Venetians, was earning its living by begging.

Throughout the nineteenth century the Venetian population remained constant at about two hundred thousand people. While most European cities were experiencing a period of industrial prosperity and population explosion, neither phenomenon touched Venice and the Venetian condition began to seem intolerable. Eventually there arose a local patriotic movement determined to expel the Austrians from Venetian territory. The remnants of the Venetian patriciate financed the movement and paper money was printed from their contributions. The 1848 revolt led by Daniele Manin enjoyed a brief success but when the Austrians succeeded in retaking the city, they built a huge bonfire to burn the abortive Republic's paper money and teach the rebellious Venetians a lesson. This gesture proved another mortal blow to the city. Venice began to deteriorate physically from the accumulating effects of over fifty years of poverty and neglect. The surviving churches, still relatively rich in artistic treasures yet deprived of the means to support themselves, took to selling off works of art simply to finance the most basic structural repairs.

---

After some twenty years' careful restoration of the interior, in 1985 the owners were still awaiting permission to restore the building's elaborate exterior.

The *portego*, or principal gallery hall, of the Palazzo Pisani-Moretta is still lit by candles set in nine eighteenth-century Murano glass chandeliers.

This was a time when great public museums and art collections were developing everywhere in Europe – London's National Gallery, Vienna's Kunsthistorisches Museum and the galleries of Berlin, Budapest and a host of other cities – and all of them acquired masterpieces of Venetian painting. At the same time private collectors were stripping Venetian palaces of furniture, *objets d'art* and entire decorative assemblages. Fragments of Venetian churches also became part of permanent museum displays all over Europe: the apse of an abandoned church on Torcello, decorated with Byzantine mosaics, was dismantled and found its way to the Kaiser Friedrich's Museum in Berlin. There is a remarkable collection of carved stone wellheads displayed in the courtyard of Budapest's Museum of Fine Arts, not to mention the fragments of Venetian sculpture that ornament country house gardens in England or the statuary from ducal tombs, like Pietro Lombardo's 'Adam', now to be found in the Metropolitan Museum of New York. The Barbarigo family sold the Czar of Russia seventeen Titians from their palace on the Grand Canal and Sir Henry Layard was able to leave London's National Gallery no fewer than nineteen important paintings including Gentile Bellini's 'Portrait of the Sultan Mohammed II' which he had bought in Venice for five pounds. In 1857 the National Gallery purchased Veronese's great 'Clemency of Alexander' from the owners of the Palazzo Pisani-Moretta.

The story of the Palazzo Pisani-Moretta can be taken to illustrate the fate of many of Venice's great houses. Shortly after the defeat of Manin's republican venture, many of the surviving patriciate retired to the country. The Pisani did just this, selling off possessions like the Veronese in order to make equitable provision for the family's heirs, and in fact none of the family returned to live in the splendid fifteenth-century Gothic palace on the Grand Canal until twelve years ago. Palazzo Pisani-Moretta lay quite uninhabited for over a century, perfectly preserved by neglect: the house was never subjected to modern improvements such as the installation of central heating, modern plumbing, gas lighting or electricity. When, in 1974, a young descendant of the family undertook to restore the house, it required three months just to clean the floor of the *sala del portego* or main hall and uncover the perfectly preserved eighteenth-century patterned terrazzo. Layer upon layer of impacted dust and grime were testimony to the time when coal-fired steam boats, the original *vaporetti*, began to ply the Grand Canal, followed by petrol-burning boats and those with diesel engines. The walls of the state apartments, with their splendid Murano glass mirrors and intricate candle sconces, surrounded by ornate Venetian stucco work, all demanded the same painstaking care, as did the delicate restoration of colourful ceiling frescos painted by Giovanni Battista Tiepolo and his followers. What emerged was a perfect example of rich, eighteenth-century Venetian décor at its most lavish. The success of the restoration is even more spectacular at night as the owner, with great sensitivity, left the nine great chandeliers in the *portego* fitted only with candles.

As certain as the success of the restoration promised to be from the outset, the Palazzo Pisani-Moretta did hold some surprises for the owner and his team of restorers. For example, when they excavated beneath the red and white marble checked flooring of the water entrance to reinforce the immense building's foundations, they discovered that the palace had been built directly on the solid earth: there was no sign of the wooden piling usually considered indispensable to secure construction on a mud-flat building site in Venice. And even with the vast size and weight of the building, Palazzo Pisani-Moretta had hardly subsided at all in five hundred years!

Little or nothing is known for certain about the foundations of Venice. It was only after the collapse of the Campanile (the bell tower of San Marco) in 1902 that engineers could examine the complete extent of one of the city's oldest building foundations. Historians debate as to whether the bell tower was begun in 888 or in 912, but in either case it had survived for almost a millennium before collapsing. The larch wood piling used to underpin the tall structure seemed to have been deployed on the principle of a raft in that relatively short lengths of piling, placed far apart, buoyed up or floated the immense weight of the building.

The disposition of later substructures in Venice was often documented, although some of the documentation has given rise to doubts if not to controversy. The most famous example is that of Baldassare Longhena's great seventeenth-century votive church, Santa Maria della Salute. Contemporary chronicles record the sinking of 1,657,000 larch wood piles over a period of two years, although experts now believe that the total number of pilings sunk in preparation for the foundations was only 110,772. By the seventeenth century, it seems that exceptionally long piles were being used to anchor the building firmly in the hard clay subsoil; the raft principle had been abandoned.

The thousand-year-old campanile of St Mark collapsed on 14 July 1902, miraculously doing no harm to any of the surrounding buildings in the Piazza San Marco. It was reconstructed ten years later.

*opposite* Seen here as it was before restoration, the Scala del Bovolo, a unique and picturesque spiral staircase built behind the Palazzo Contarini del Bovolo.

It comes as something of a surprise to find that larch wood will become petrified in the lagoon's partially brackish water and that the wooden piling foundations of Venice can consequently be as hard as the rock of Manhattan island. During the recent restoration of the eighteenth-century Jesuit church in the city's northern quarter, the steel bits of the modern drilling equipment broke on the ancient wooden piling of the building's foundations. What is only just beginning to be understood now, two decades after the 1966 flood, is that exceptionally low tides are potentially more harmful to Venetian buildings than the spectacular *acqua alta* because contact with the air may rot the exposed heads of Venice's larch wood piling and undermine foundations. This was partly the problem at the Jesuit church, although an even more precarious situation had resulted from the position of the church's apse and eastern walls built flush on the edge of a wide canal. This canal emptied out into the lagoon only a hundred feet or so away from the building and its exceptional width tended to increase the force of the tidal ebb and flow from the lagoon, creating strong

currents that were threatening the building's structural stability. Early in this century, large fissures appeared in the cornices of the apse. The cracked stonework was pinned together with great iron clamps which effectively prevented the apse from breaking away from the building and sliding into the canal. But with the passage of time, Venice's salt sea air rusted and corroded the iron clamps, so that one of the two was completely eaten away. Catastrophe seemed imminent but was averted by the timely contributions of the American Save Venice, Inc. committee. Engineers were able to secure the foundations of the church's east wall and apse in a brace of reinforced concrete piling.

---

The elegant interior of a clandestine eighteenth-century casino, the Ridotto della Procuratoressa Venier, restored by the French Committee.

The great Gothic church of SS. Giovanni and Paolo, before which stands perhaps the most magnificent equestrian statue in the world – the *condottiere* Bartolomeo Colleoni by Andrea Verrochio.

The Jesuit church was one of the most extravagant baroque buildings constructed in eighteenth-century Venice. The numerous members of the Order were housed in an enormous complex next to the church which, under the Napoleonic regime, became a military barracks. The Benedictine convent at San Zaccaria and the Palladian complex of monastic buildings on the island of San Giorgio Maggiore suffered the same fate. Although the church and its monastic orders were impoverished by the suppressions and confiscations ordered by Napoleon, it is seldom realized that successive occupying powers pursued precisely the same policy. The Catholic Austrians did not restore property to the monastic orders, nor did the Unification of Italy under the House of Savoy much improve the situation of the church. The first King of United Italy died excommunicate for his seizure of ecclesiastical property. Countless island monasteries were adopted as powder magazines by the military while others, following the model of the Republic's Lazar Houses, were transformed into isolation hospitals and asylums. The Franciscans' cloister, known as the Ca' Grande at the Frari, eventually became the principal repository of the Venetian state archives while the vast complex built to house over five hundred Dominican monks at SS. Giovanni e Paolo, was used as the Civic Hospital of the Veneto Province. The suppressed conventual church of the Augustinians at the Carità became the Academy of Fine Arts with the Gallery of Paintings housed in the adjacent *scuola* and conventual buildings, and the Benedictines' church of San Gregorio was used first as a military depot, then as a storehouse and tobacco factory. The beautiful Gothic abbey buildings enclose what Ruskin called 'the most beautiful courtyard in Venice', long abandoned, partly demolished and, since the last war, used as a private house.

At least these buildings survived the nineteenth century. Their properties and vast holdings were confiscated and they were stripped of their treasures – altars, paintings, furniture, statuary and crucifixes, reliquaries, funerary monuments and the like – but they were spared the fate of the more than eighty churches and convents which were razed to the ground during the seven years of Napoleon's imperial regime. The same brief period, during which Napoleon fulfilled his promise to be an Attila for the Venetian state also saw the demolition of forty palaces. Many others suffered the fate of the Palazzo Pisani-Moretta and

---

After the prohibition by the Austrian authorities of further burials in the city itself, the cemetery island of San Michele became the city's chief burial ground.

were simply abandoned after the failure of Manin's Republic and the final collapse of the Venetian economy.

At long last, the Austrians began to make a half-hearted attempt to conserve what was left. They showed concern for the health of the lagoon city's inhabitants by filling in some of the more stagnant canals and creating the *rio terà* or earthed-in canals that resemble broad streets in other cities. At the same time they forbad burial in the churches and cloisters and created that extraordinary Island of the Dead, San Michele, where the poor lie interred for a decade before their bones are exhumed and removed to an ossuary island, thus freeing the grave site for another generation. (The bones of the rich are housed in the island's many mausolea.)

The Austrians made another provision for Venice that was to change its character forever. The railway, that symbol of nineteenth-century progress and prosperity, was brought into the very heart of the city by the construction of a three-and-a-half-mile-long rail causeway built across the lagoon. For the first time in its millennial existence, Venice was inextricably bound to the mainland and ceased to be an island. The church of Santa Lucia and the Scuola dei Nobili were torn down to make way for a new railway station and an iron bridge was thrown across the Grand Canal at a point nearby. The Austrians then built a second iron bridge over the Grand Canal at the Accademia. All of this construction was carried out in a modern industrial style hardly suited to its setting amid buildings some two to three hundred years old. Fortunately, because the Austrians still favoured Trieste over Venice for improvement and development, these new buildings were relatively few and far between in the city. In any case, they represented the aggressive, pompous taste of all nineteenth-century Europe and cannot be blamed solely on the Austrians. Indeed, Venice's own town council showed itself all too anxious to improve the city at the expense of its former beauty. In 1858 it passed a resolution, with only a few dissenting votes, to tear down all the old buildings on the Riva degli Schiavoni overlooking the San Marco Basin and build there a gigantic international exposition centre of the Crystal Palace sort, beloved of nineteenth-century Europe. But despite the town council's vote of approval, the project was never realized: it simply cost too much for a city of Venice's extremely limited financial resources. Today's opponents of the mammoth project to close off the lagoon with moveable barriers might take comfort from this little cautionary tale now a hundred years old.

In certain instances, the Austrians did show respect for Venice's past, but not always in ways that benefited the city. Their passion for history and documentation, for example, led them to confiscate the entire Venetian state archive and transfer it to Vienna for study and cataloguing. They also set about restoring two historic buildings which survive today as evidence of the rather doubtful aesthetic and scientific criteria of mid-nineteenth-century restoration work. Both of these projects were partly inspired by the enthusiasm and polemic of John Ruskin whose masterpiece, *The Stones of Venice*, would influence the Englishman's attitude to Venice for the next century. It was he who called the authorities' attention to the delapidated condition of two examples of Venice's earliest architecture.

The first of the Austrians' two projects was not really a restoration, but rather an extremely dubious reconstruction. The Venetian town council had purchased the Fondaco dei Turchi on the Grand Canal after the death of the last Turkish merchant to live there. This horribly decaying structure had been built as a palace in the early thirteenth century and was one of the oldest surviving examples of Venetian domestic architecture. The restorers began by clearing its interior of the rooms that centuries of Turkish merchants had used for the storage

A photograph taken in the 1850s, showing the dilapidated thirteenth-century house of the Pesaro family, usually known as the Fondaco dei Turchi from its ancient use as a Turkish merchants' emporium and residence.

of their merchandise, as baths, a harem and even a mosque and set about reconstructing the marble-encrusted façade of an early Veneto-Byzantine-style palace. The whole exercise was academic in the extreme as the harshly modern result, hardly mellowed after a hundred years, still indicates.

The second of the two major restoration projects undertaken by the Austrians, that of Murano's cathedral church of Santa Maria e San Donato, is characterized by the same, coldly mechanical appearance, largely caused by the machinery used for cutting the stonework. The heavy-handed treatment cannot be blamed entirely on the Austrians, however, as by the time it was completed in 1873, Venice had become an integral part of the Kingdom of United Italy. The Risorgimento, and especially its romantic heroes, Garibaldi, Cavour and the King, Vittorio Emmanuele, had proved extremely popular abroad and the English and other

The reconstruction of the Fondaco dei Turchi carried out by Federico Berchet in 1858–69 has been universally disparaged although it offers a fairly valid synthesis of the Veneto-Byzantine style.

foreigners were attracted not only to visit, but to invest in the New Italy. The economic possibilities of Venice, or rather, Murano, captured the imagination of Sir Henry Layard, an eminent Victorian who, in 1868, founded the Venezia and Murano Glass and Mosaic Works. His firm, ably managed by Signor Salviati, obtained a contract for the maintenance of San Marco's mosaics and the restoration of the great mosaic cycle in Torcello's cathedral. The recent consolidation of the latter revealed the high quality of the Salviati restoration.

Layard's attempt to revive the fortunes of Murano found a counterpart on other islands in the lagoon. New sea-bathing establishments brought a summer season of tourism to the Lido, while the Stucky grain mills built on the Giudecca island in 1884 introduced a modern industrial complex into the centre of the city. The Contessa Andrianna Marcello revived the art of lace-making among the orphan girls on Burano. These attempts to create modern industries in Venice proved relatively short-lived. The taste for Venetian lacework and

The broad sandy shore of the Lido was developed in the late nineteenth century when deserted dunes and pine forests gave way to grand hotels such as that seen in *Death in Venice*.

decoration in mosaic did not survive the end of the nineteenth century and Stucky's vast mills met the fate of all such enterprises as the new century dawned. The *fin de siècle* atmosphere of the city at that time has been captured, if grimly so, by Thomas Mann in his haunting novella, *Death in Venice* while, at virtually the same time, Marcel Proust and Gabriele d'Annunzio were luxuriating in the style available to the happy few fortunate enough to lodge in Danieli's Hotel on the Riva, to pass the time in Florian's on the Piazza or to make luxury purchases from the great Spanish dress designer and painter, Mariano Fortuny. But by comparison with the rest of Italy, where a solid industrial wealth was spreading through railways, land reclamation, Milan's growing steel and textile industries and the nascent automobile industry of Turin, Venice was still excruciatingly poor. Of course, its poverty had preserved it to perfection and there were those who appreciated its beauty and even profited from it. At the very end of the nineteenth century, the young Bernard Berenson published his first volume of art historical studies, *The Venetian Painters of the Renaissance*, laying the groundwork for his long and fascinating career as a connoisseur. It was a career which enabled him to locate and purchase great works of Venetian art on behalf of rich American and English collectors, once again turning Venice's poverty to enrich the world.

50

# The Twentieth-Century Siege

THE TWENTIETH CENTURY HAS EMERGED as the natural enemy of Venice and by the end of its second decade, the seeds were sown that might have reaped the city's annihilation in our own day. Certainly the contrasts between the century and the city could not be greater. Whereas war twice engulfed and almost overwhelmed Europe in the first fifty years, Venice has increasingly become a haven of peace and tranquillity. It is a city remarkable for the human scale of its construction while the rest of the world today favours skyscrapers and giantism in engineering. And Venice accommodates the human pace of life – even horses were officially banned from the centre over six hundred years ago – in an age that values speed and efficiency, rocketing into outer space where calculations are made in light years, not human years; an age that wants instant computerized communication and information. Venice encourages the arts and crafts where other cities develop their industries on an inhuman scale, and all too frequently in inhuman conditions. (In this context, an official health report submitted to the Italian government in 1979 estimated that it would cost the government less to remove the entire population of Mestre-Marghera a safe distance from the petro-chemical refinery complex there than to build hospitals sufficient to cope with the lung diseases bound to be caused by the polluted air in the area.) The twentieth century seeks reassurance from what it regards as science's certainties and history's facts while Venice has always delighted in legend and in the constantly changing realities of the marketplace. Venice's artistic treasures survive, in the city and abroad, as a witness to her powers of creation while the twentieth century's most significant contribution to the arts of civilization seems to be the unrivalled ability to preserve relics of the past.

Early in the twentieth century, the government of the Kingdom of United Italy took measures to alleviate Venice's poverty. With Trieste in Austrian hands, Venice became Italy's most important Adriatic naval base and warships were built, once again, on an impressive scale in the Arsenal dockyards. Of course, all this activity drew fire in the First World War and visitors to Venice are often surprised to come across plaques commemorating Austrian artillery hits in the city. A number of Venetian churches were bombarded, including the church of Santa Croce, which gives its name to one of the city's six *sestieri*, and the church of the Discalced Carmelites near the railway station where part of the great ceiling fresco by Giovanni Battista Tiepolo was destroyed. Venice was in a vulnerable position and, following the Italian army retreat from Caporetto, the situation became critical. Villas on the Venetian mainland, being even closer to the front lines, were requisitioned to serve as hospitals and their frescoed interiors were whitewashed to render them more suitably hygienic as hospital wards. Two of Andrea Palladio's greatest architectural masterpieces succumbed to this fate but after the war, both found new owners who set about restoring the fresco cycles. The frescoed rooms of the Villa Foscari at Malcontenta, ten miles from Venice, underwent an exemplary restoration but never regained their original richness of colour. The wonderful Veronese cycle of frescos in the Villa Barbaro at Maser was rather more radically restored and this is evident under a raking light, when it is easy to see the scoring in the walls necessary to make whitewash adhere to a frescoed surface. Although such treatment of Veronese's masterpieces may seem barbarous, it is salutary to remember, in these days of the

---

Venice is a city of extraordinary contrasts, twentieth-century living juxtaposed with relics of past centuries such as the stones (below and opposite) so beloved of John Ruskin. The stone paterae, carved as votive plaques with religious motifs, often date back to the Byzantine era.

indiscriminate worship of art, that the loss of a few paintings or statues is never too high a price to pay to save the lives of soldiers dying in the defence of their country.

In the very last year of the First World War, an Italian entrepreneur of extraordinary genius, the man who later bought and restored the Villa Barbaro at Maser, succeeded in bringing all the twentieth century's creative power and productive potential right to the edge of the Venetian lagoon in an attempt to rescue Venice from her condition of paralyzing poverty. It is difficult for us to imagine now exactly how impoverished Venice still was in 1917-18. The ultimate victory of the Allies brought no benefits to a stagnated backwater town – indeed, the enemy attack had come so close to Venice that the Italian Navy decided to transfer its shipbuilding activities to Genoa and Naples, a safer distance from enemy borders. The Venetian population still hovered around two hundred thousand, the same it had been a hundred years earlier when it matched the size of European cities like Vienna and Berlin. But now these cities, even though decimated by the war and sunk in defeat, numbered their inhabitants in the millions.

In 1917, a consortium of Venetian investors headed by Count Giuseppe Volpi purchased large tracts of unreclaimed marshland on the lagoon's western edge. No one lived in this inhospitable terrain, save for the villagers of Mestre some distance away. The only landmark was the deserted fortress at Marghera, last used during the Austrian occupation some fifty years before. Volpi realized that this marshland could be reclaimed and made suitably solid for development by using Venice's traditional piling to reinforce the embankments. The important feature of this marshy shoreline was that it was cut through and crossed by a number of deep-water channels. In fact, part of Volpi's intention was to restore Venice's past prosperity as a centre of maritime commerce. The novelty of his vision consisted in using the land reclaimed near Marghera not as the site of a conventional port, but as an area where refineries and factories could be built. Raw materials would arrive by ship – still the most economical means of long-distance transport – and be unloaded directly into the appropriate factory or refinery. There would be no need to unload at a conventional port and then pay the costs of further overland shipment to a distant refinery or processing plant. Volpi's conception proved so profitable that within the first year of the industrial port's operation, its users found that they had cut their costs by fully ninety per cent.

The original idea of the Marghera industrial port has now been transformed beyond recognition, but that did not come about for another forty years, until after the Second World War. Between the two wars industrial expansion was steady, although slow by comparison with the economic boom that followed the Second World War. Venetians continued to cross the lagoon to their new jobs at Marghera using the rail causeway built by the Austrians; they still lived in Venice in the houses of their ancestors. Count Volpi and his principal partners, Count Cini and Ingeniere Gaggia, sought to facilitate this pattern of commuting by having a road bridge built alongside the rail causeway and thus making a bus service feasible. This final, and ultimately more disastrous, link with the mainland was completed only fifty years ago, in 1933. Once this major bridgehead had been established, the twentieth century's direct assault on Venice began to accelerate rapidly.

By this time Count Volpi had become Mussolini's Minister of Finance while Cini was nominated a Senator of the Realm. Both men participated in sundry business and financial enterprises throughout Italy and the rest of pre-war Europe. They drew attention to Venice through their patronage of the Venice Biennale, the biannual international exhibition of

Viewed from the campanile of the Frari, the road and rail links that so nearly proved the city's undoing by siphoning off the working population from the *centro storico* to the industrial mainland.

---

contemporary art, and their sponsorship of the newly created Venice Film Festival. It was in Venice that Mussolini chose to welcome his newfound admirer, Adolf Hitler, to Italy in 1933.

Oddly enough, none of these episodes in recent Venetian history had much permanent effect on the city and its condition as a provincial backwater. The Biennale and the Film Festival still exist, it is true, and they attract publicity and bring prestige to Venice, but they have fallen into the hands of politicians and bureaucrats from Rome and bring very little permanent benefit to the city. Hitler's brutal friendship with Mussolini was disastrous for all of Italy although Venice was spared the worst consequences. Long before Hitler's visit, Mussolini recognized the fundamental indifference of Venice to political fanaticism and never attempted to stage any of his monstrous propaganda rallies in the city. Even in the tragic period after 1943, when the dreaded Nazi-Fascist Republic of Saló was established in the Veneto, Venice remained aloof and the city became a sanctuary and refuge for mainland Jews escaping from Hitler's quotas for deportation. In the end, even history conspired with geography to respect Venice's tradition of inviolate sanctuary and the war was over by the time the Allied armies reached the lagoon. The very first Allied arrivals, like Colonel 'Popsky' who drove a jeep around the Piazza San Marco in exultation, often found themselves seated next to German officers in mufti enjoying a last glass of champagne before returning home to face the firing squad or the denazification trials.

The year of Hitler and Mussolini's first encounter, 1933, witnessed a significant change in the structure of Venetian life that many see as the crux of the Venetian problem today. The

55

local authorities decided to bind Marghera's increasing prosperity to its Venetian parent by extending Venice's municipal jurisdiction to include Marghera and its factories as well as some of the neighbouring villages where a few of the workers had gone to live. Henceforth the Mayor of Venice would be the Mayor of Marghera and Mestre, too, just as after 1886 he had become the Mayor of the Lido. The rail and road bridges served as a symbol of this political link between the mainland and what began to be called the 'centro storico', or historic centre. Shortly before his death in 1977, Count Vittorio Cini, then well over ninety years old, remarked that if he could have foreseen the calamity that the bridge represented, he would have dismantled it stone by stone with his own hands.

Vittorio Cini was a remarkable man and the story of his life definitely belongs to any account of Venice preserved. Exercising his genius in partnership with Giuseppe Volpi, he emerged as one of pre-war Europe's most impressive businessmen and industrialists. Following the success of the Marghera industrial port, Cini and his partners helped organize the giant national cartels characteristic of Fascist economic theory and still the backbone of Italian industry and finance. Among the better known abroad were the Italian and Adriatic shipping companies and the CIGA luxury hotel chain, with its headquarters purposefully located in Venice. They also created a company to supply all of northern Italy with electricity along with a number of other public service companies that were eventually nationalized. One of the richest, and most successful entrepreneurs in Europe, Cini was also a loyal servant of the state, serving as a Senator in the Parliament of the Kingdom. When, in September 1943, Vittorio Emmanuele III had his Prime Minister, Benito Mussolini, placed under arrest and imprisoned, Cini and Volpi both declared their loyalty to the King.

As history relates, both Mussolini's arrest and the King's surrender of Italy to the Allies turned out to be dead-letter technicalities. The Allies were too suspicious to advance up the Italian peninsula from Anzio and occupy the capital and their hesitation gave the Germans time to rescue Mussolini from prison and send their own armies south to Rome. The King fled to the safety of the Allied camp in Cairo and the Germans established Mussolini as their puppet dictator of a Nazi-Fascist republic on the shores of Lake Garda at Salò. Any Italian soldiers and officers who remained loyal to the King and refused to join the German armies were shot and since the Germans could hardly count on the undivided loyalty of any troops remaining in Italy, they were all sent, miserably ill-equipped for the coming winter, to join the German forces on the Russian front.

There was also a price placed on the heads of all Fascist ministers and government officials who had conspired for the overthrow of Mussolini and declared loyalty to the King after the Duce's arrest. Count Volpi escaped to Switzerland but Count Cini was arrested and, like the King's own daughter, the Princess of Hesse, sent to a concentration camp in Germany. Cini's only son, Giorgio, courageously went directly to Berlin and bargained with the Gestapo for his father's release. As he negotiated he pushed diamond bracelets and necklaces across the conference table and watched as the German officers took them, in silence, and put them in their uniform jacket pockets. After days of these nerve-wracking encounters, Giorgio Cini was informed that he could proceed to Dachau near Munich and his father would be released to him. The Gestapo kept their word and Giorgio was able to escort his father to safety in Switzerland.

After the war, Count Cini returned to his business interests and contributed to the reconstruction of Italy. Then, in 1949, in the company of his son's fiancée, the cinema actress

The island of San Giorgio Maggiore, whose restoration was financed by industrialist Vittorio Cini between 1952 and 1954.

Merle Oberon, he watched Giorgio take off in his small plane at Cannes airport and crash at the end of the runway. Cini was shattered by the death of his only son, the young man who had saved his life. Always a devout Catholic, he underwent a spiritual crisis and, returning to Venice, decided to devote his fortune and energies to creating a philanthropic foundation in memory of Giorgio. For this purpose he leased from the Italian government the island of San Giorgio Maggiore with its great Palladian church and the vast monastic complex that had been suppressed and despoiled in 1807 and for the intervening 150 years served successive occupying powers as a military base.

This apparently endless and humiliating military occupation had reduced the island of San Giorgio Maggiore to the condition of a wasteland. Its buildings had been gutted and rearranged to suit the various armies and then progressively deserted and abandoned as the garrisons were reduced in strength. The deterioration and delapidation were impressive and the odds against the island ever recovering its former glory seemed strong indeed. But anyone who has seen a Canaletto of the Basin of San Marco or stood in the Piazzetta and looked across the water will understand the beauty that beckoned to be rescued and preserved. And anyone who has since been present at the innumerable conferences, conventions, lectures, symposia or international summit meetings or who has attended one of the sung masses in the church, the concerts in the cloisters, the ballet performances in the Teatro Verde or the exhibitions of Venetian art in the abbatial apartments, or consulted the splendid collections in the rich seventeenth-century library, will understand something of the success of Count Cini's undertaking. Only from the tall bell tower can one fully understand the scope of his achievement and wonder that one man's vision could be so inspired and that such a man could personally direct its successful realization in only two years. Apart from the cloisters inhabited by the Giorgio Cini Foundation of Venetian Culture and Civilization and

*above* The courtyard of San Giorgio Maggiore, now part of the Giorgio Cini Foundation of Venetian Culture and Civilization, one of the finest centres of scholarship in Europe. The church itself, originally suppressed by Napoleon, was returned to the Benedictine Order in 1954.

*opposite* The restored seventeenth-century monastic library which houses many rich collections.

the acres of newly planted gardens that surround them, there is a vocational school and an institute where the orphan sons of merchant sailors are taught the rudiments of maritime skills.

Palladio's magnificent church was returned to the care of the Benedictine Order and the activities of the Fondazione were inaugurated in 1954. In retrospect, it is astonishing that Cini's extraordinary accomplishment did not immediately encourage the local authorities to restore Venice's innumerable deteriorating and derelict monuments. But the reason for the persistent indifference and the resulting deterioration can be sought again in the rail and road bridge that Count Cini had wanted to demolish with his own bare hands. Just as Venice had been threatened throughout the nineteenth century with a slow, lingering death due to impoverishment and neglect, now its life and continued existence were to be threatened by post-war prosperity and an agonizing abandonment. And it was this situation that was to prevail right down to the crises of November 1966 and 1967.

# Undermining the Last Defences

PROSPERITY CAME IN THE WAKE OF Italy's amazing recovery from the ravages of the Second World War. In Venice, the 'Italian economic miracle' meant the expansion of Marghera's industrial facilities. With this expansion came speculators who bought up acres of what had been farmland on the outskirts of Mestre and built cheap apartment blocks for Marghera's factory and refinery workers. This conveniently situated housing was particularly attractive to the Venetians who had been commuting to work by *vaporetto* up the Grand Canal to the Piazzale Roma bus terminal and across the road bridge to the mainland – a journey that might take up to an hour or more. But the new apartments offered other attractions besides a convenient location. Although many of the buildings were obviously jerry-built, they did come equipped with all the so-called modern comforts. Pride of place was given to central heating, a relative novelty in post-war Italy and definitely a novelty for the Venetian working classes whose ancient houses in the Castello and Cannaregio districts of the historic centre had never been heated with more than coal – or wood-burning kitchen stoves.

After the war, Italians everywhere were tempted by the glamorous promises of the economic miracle. Other Italian cities provided cheap housing in nineteenth-century apartment buildings located in the outskirts or else in the more modern workers' quarters constructed under Fascist rule. Venice had nothing at all of this sort; the city did not even have an outskirts or periphery. Her working classes lived in the houses of their forbears while the poorest sought shelter in the dark, insalubrious, ground-floor storerooms of palaces owned by absentee landlords unaware of their existence. A landlord who registered his palace as an uninhabitable warehouse paid no taxes on it. Several of Venice's most important historic palaces are still maintained in that category today. Such buildings have no modern plumbing,

The Rio di San Salvatore emptied for dredging. The dampcourse of Istrian stone on the left marks the normal watermark.

*above* The *traghetto* or gondola ferry service crosses the Grand Canal at half a dozen points. The boats are larger than the normal gondola and the passengers traditionally remain standing.

*opposite* Venice today: (above left) a tenement in the Campo Santa Margherita, condemned to picturesque decay by the city's paralyzing restoration laws; (above right) a minor palazzo awaiting the restorer; (below) past and present, the ornamental and the strictly functional, side by side in this typical roofscape.

---

let alone central heating. In fact, forty-five per cent of houses in Venice today are without a bathroom and their inhabitants have no option but to resort to the public baths. The toilet, behind a screen or curtain in the kitchen, drains through a pipe directly into the canal outside. Fully sixty-five per cent of Venetian drains empty into the city's canals.

For centuries this was the norm for life in Venice. The canals were swept clean twice a day by the tide waters which, crossing the lagoon's shoals from the shallow Adriatic, have the highest salt and oxygen content of any sea in the world. Such geological quirks maintained an ecological balance between man and nature that kept Venice a perfectly healthy city throughout its long history. The Plague was an epidemic imported from abroad and the Venetians tried to defend themselves from it with the invention of quarantine: forty days of isolation for ships' crews arriving from infested ports. Today the plague that threatens the health of Venice's natural setting comes not from abroad, but from the chemicals in detergents, fertilizers and plastic packaging used daily in the city and on the mainland. Yet the ecological balance, although increasingly precarious, has been maintained to date. Venetian children can still swim in the canal on the hottest sirocco days while the menfolk fish from the city's bridges.

The delights of life in the streets and squares of the world's most beautiful city were hardly adequate compensation for the condition into which Venice's minor housing had fallen by the 1950s. All the city's buildings bore the scars of a hundred and fifty years of impoverishment and neglect and the houses of the poorly paid working classes had naturally suffered more than most. Although many Venetians were eventually driven away from the city by the inexorable deterioration of their houses, an increasing determination on the part of the authorities to preserve the monuments of the historic centre was also threatening to make Venice uninhabitable. Some of the earliest, serious preservation laws had been enacted under the Fascist regime in an attempt to capture the reflected glory of an otherwise vanished past. After the war, the Italian Republic followed suit as speculators and the modern taste in building seemed on the verge of bringing about the indiscriminate destruction of Italy's architectural heritage. Some of the most offensive examples of this modern barbarism are to be found in Venice. In the same year as San Giorgio Maggiore's restoration, the entire side of a square in the city's centre (adjacent to the seventeenth-century church of San Moisè) was demolished, a street filled in and a public bridge torn down in order to clear a building site for an enormous hotel whose aggressively modern façade is still a discordant note in an otherwise remarkably harmonious townscape. A similar modern hotel extension was allowed to rise on the Riva degli Schiavoni overlooking the San Marco Basin, at the expense of buildings that Canaletto once considered sufficiently picturesque to include in his finest compositions. Fortunately, there have been relatively few of these modern excrescences permitted in Venice and the outcry against them was sufficient to reactivate the city's few preservation laws. But these laws primarily concerned the preservation of old buildings and the prohibition of inappropriate modern building was no more than implicit. The only useful criterion for determining legally which buildings should be preserved remains that of age. Hence over ninety-five per cent of Venice's buildings qualify as Historical Monuments.

This legal definition means that the majority of householders are unable to modernize their properties, for the law not only prohibits alterations to the exterior of any historic monument, but also to the interior. You can no more install a modern bathroom in a delapidated Venetian working-class house than you could introduce such a convenience into the Palazzo Pitti's grandest gilded ballroom. No matter how small and lacking in architectural distinction or even significant ornament, by virtue of its age – usually some two to three hundred years old in the case of the most recent construction in the historic centre – the Venetian working-class house is nonetheless classified an historic monument and, as such, placed forever in the same category of protection with the Palazzo Pitti and other such national treasures.

Of course, the authorities have always made it technically possible to alter an historic monument, but in order to do so the owner has to hire a lawyer to make the formal requests, a surveyor to document the current state of the building and an architect to draw up plans to be submitted, through the lawyer, for approval. Permission has to be obtained for the installation of main drains, for example, and given the high percentage of drains already emptying into Venice's canals, this permission is granted only very infrequently. Much of

---

*Pages 64-5* Daily life in Venice.

# UNDERMINING THE LAST DEFENCES

Venice's housing drainage today has been installed illegally. But even with all the appropriate permits in order, the owner often has to face the extremely high costs of construction work on a building where one or more of the walls rises from the water. The cost of scaffolding in Italy is exorbitant and to erect it on a canal wall is virtually prohibitive. Installing a bathroom apart, any internal improvement is liable to involve the building's basic structure – especially since the majority of Venetian buildings have not been subject to regular maintenance since the fall of the Republic almost two hundred years ago.

The difficulties of modernizing, or even improving, a Venetian house are legion and for the poorer working-class Venetian in the 'fifties and 'sixties, they proved overwhelming. So with the offer of an attractive alternative in Mestre's modern housing developments, Venetians began to desert the historic centre. The post-war population numbered about 170,000 Venetians. Today there are under half that number left in the city and it is estimated that only 20,000 of them had parents and grandparents born in Venice. Although the city may no longer be sinking, this terrible depopulation has not yet been halted. Venice's lifeblood is being drained away as the young and able-bodied leave behind a population with the highest average age of any European city. And there is an extremely high proportion of uninhabited housing because much of what the young have abandoned is virtually uninhabitable, so there is also a housing shortage in a city built for twice the number who

---

The price exacted by the tourist industry, mainstay of the city's finances, can be heavy on the fabric. This is the Ponte della Paglia, just one of 345 public bridges demanding constant maintenance.

The early morning market at the Rialto with typical Venetian barges unloading fresh fish.

actually live there. Of the 85,000 Venetians still living in the historic centre in 1985, fully 28,000 commute to jobs on the mainland, while Mestre and its satellites send 12,000 back into the city every day. Few people realize how many gondoliers, water-taxi drivers, glass blowers and their apprentices, waiters in restaurants, butchers, bakers and other neighbourhood tradesmen, like the greengrocer at the local stall, choose to live on the mainland rather than in Venice itself.

The depopulation has also had serious consequences for the fabric of the city. Venetian building has deteriorated to the point where it has taken a concerted effort on the part of the local government, the provincial government, the regional government, the national government, a United Nations agency and more than thirty international committees in order to preserve the city. At the same time, the migration away from the historic centre transformed Mestre-Marghera and their surroundings into a substantial community of some four hundred thousand Venetians and the Venice municipal administration found itself in the invidious position of having to spend the funds created by taxes where the voters were living. A perfectly justifiable strategy, but one which virtually represented a policy of neglect for the historic centre. Mestre acquired much needed amenities with public money: paved

The neo-Gothic arcades of the fish market, designed and built in 1907, incorporate fragments of ancient Venetian buildings.

streets, street lighting and main drainage for newly constructed housing developments; new public transport networks; new schools, churches and community centres, etc., etc., etc., while the requirements of the historic centre were constantly being shelved or postponed for 'lack of funds'.

Le Corbusier called Venice 'the city of the Future', but keeping it in order is an art that belongs to the past and simple jobs of day-to-day maintenance in Venice are certainly more complicated and expensive than in conventional cities. Le Corbusier's paradoxical assertion referred to his theory that (as in his conception of the ideal city of the future) residential and commercial traffic should be separated or allowed to circulate on two different levels. He took Venice's canals to represent the commercial artery in his ideal scheme.

As has been mentioned, the Austrian administration tried to maintain healthy circulation in the city's canal network by filling in those that had silted up or become stagnant. The tendency to shoal or silt up exists everywhere in the Venetian lagoon and many of the city's twenty-four miles of canals need dredging from time to time. Coffer dams are built across either end of a section of canal and the water is pumped out for the dredging. It is a slow and expensive operation, but an essential and regular part of maintenance in the city and one that was woefully neglected during the worst period of depopulation when Mestre expanded at Venice's expense. Draining the canals is essential not just for reasons of hygiene but because it gives landlords an opportunity to examine and repair the foundations of their buildings. Twenty years have passed since the city last provided this opportunity and by the time the current draining and dredging programme is completed in 1995, a full thirty years will have elapsed, a very long period of neglect for buildings built in Venetian conditions. Meanwhile the complicated networks of piping and drainage beneath the city's thoroughfares must be specially maintained as they are under constant attack from the lagoon's salt water. When sections of pavement are torn up to repair some conduit, the paving stone must be recut and relaid by hand, a process which requires skills of an order quite different from those of road menders spreading asphalt. The Istrian stone steps leading down to the water, or the quayside edging in the same material, all require hand finishing, not to mention the plain stone stanchions or the fancier details on some of Venice's 345 public bridges. The bridges themselves, often subjected to terrific daily assault by tourists, must be reinforced and occasionally rebuilt, again requiring superior masons and bricklayers skilled in the construction of arches – workers that would never be found on the municipal payroll of most twentieth-century cities.

The Accademia Bridge is probably the most obvious example of the neglect and indifference characteristic of the city's recent history. The bridge was designed in 1933 as a temporary structure made of wood to replace the Austrians' iron bridge. In the fifty years since, no project for a permanent bridge, like the stone one at the railway station, has ever been adopted and the condition of the wooden bridge, which has come to seem less and less temporary to the Venetians, has deteriorated to such an extent that in 1984, it was decided to dismantle it altogether. When the operation began, there was actually no approved plan for the bridge's reconstruction. The old iron underpinnings and reinforcements would remain in place as a skeleton until the authorities agreed on an acceptable design – a most unsatisfactory state of affairs which meant there could be no question either of calculating the necessarily escalating cost to the taxpayer, or of naming the date when the bridge would reopen to Venetian traffic.

In the 1960s, the picture of Venice was a depressing one. A city deserted by its inhabitants and neglected by local administrators determined to meet the needs of a much larger constituency elsewhere. A city of abandoned and delapidated housing. And the condition of the city as one of Europe's cultural and artistic capitals was equally distressing. The Superintendent of the Galleries and the Superintendent of Monuments faced problems in Venice that were typical of jurisdictions in cities all over Italy. There was always a shortage of funds. Museum entrance fees collected in a major cultural capital like Florence would be forwarded to Rome for redistribution in the Tuscan province. Small provincial museums, with only a handful of visitors each year, were effectively subsidized by the crowds visiting great galleries like the Uffizi. Consequently, after the costs of upkeep had been met, the Uffizi would never have sufficient resources to employ an adequate staff, let alone to embark on a time-consuming and hence expensive programme of restoration and maintenance. Much of the gallery was frequently closed to the public and important paintings had to be stored away because there was not enough money to install the necessary burglar alarms or climatic controls or to hang and light them properly in the available gallery space. These were problems encountered by all Italy's major galleries, particularly in the post-war decades,

The Accademia Bridge, built of wood in 1933 to replace the original iron bridge of 1854 which proved too low for the *vaporetti* to pass beneath it. Pronounced unsafe in 1984, it is now undergoing long-overdue repairs.

---

before the advent of mass tourism and the recent widespread popularity of art history. In 1949 the Uffizi sold a hundred thousand admission tickets while in 1980 there were one and a half million visitors to the gallery.

If the Uffizi, which at one time charged the highest entrance fee of any public gallery in Europe, found itself short of funds with which to care for its collection, the situation in Venice was far worse. Venice's paintings, like her buildings, had suffered too long from impoverishment and neglect. Florence's period of Austrian occupation had transformed the city into the prosperous, well-administered capital of a semi-independent Habsburg duchy. And this was followed by a full five years as the capital of the Kingdom of United Italy when patriotism combined with prosperity expressed itself in new building and the 'restoration' of the monuments of the past. One need only think of the gigantic, costly marble façades created for the Duomo and Santa Croce in the nineteenth century to have a picture of Florence's flourishing condition when Venice was still stagnating as a backwater town of the Austrian provinces. In the post-war years, while Florence sought to conserve the Uffizi and

A large mirror for barge traffic on the Rio Ognisanti solves the problem of a blind intersection of Venetian canals.

Pitti Gallery collections along with scattered masterpieces of the Florentine fifteenth-century Renaissance, the Venetian authorities had to begin with twelfth-century treasures, surviving on a scale unequalled anywhere in Europe, and try to preserve the works of art produced by an unbroken tradition of a full five hundred years. In addition, the two Venetian Superintendents had charge of a jurisdiction that included the whole of the Veneto Province as well as other territories. It was too much to be able to do justice to all that needed preservation.

After the 1966 and 1967 floodings, when the sad state of Venetian art works and monuments received worldwide attention, the two Superintendents sought to have their jurisdictions redefined and limited to the historic centre and the islands. This unprecedented bureaucratic restructuring took some time to achieve, but when it finally came about in 1978, the two Superintendents became known as the Superintendent of the Artistic and Historic Heritage and the Superintendent of the Architectural Heritage and the Environment. For the early part of the campaign to safeguard Venice, and Venetian works of art, their work was done under the more convenient and descriptive titles of Superintendent of Galleries and

Two sandoli being prepared for the tourist trade: their carpets and protective canvas covers are given an airing while the boatman polishes the sleek black chairs of his boat.

---

Superintendent of Monuments. But quite apart from the impossibly extensive scope of their jurisdiction the Superintendents were consistently hampered by the lack of funds. This was the area in which the foreign committees organized after the 1966 floods made their first important contributions.

# Relief: Paintings Restored

T HE CHEQUERED HISTORY OF ONE RESTORATION laboratory in particular provides an excellent illustration of the kind of logistic problems that faced the pioneers in the early phases of the campaign to rescue Venetian art. Before the 1966 flood, the Superintendent of the Galleries had been obliged to send the larger Venetian oil paintings outside the city for restoration. This was particularly unsatisfactory for a number of reasons. Since the fifteenth century, Venetian art has been characterized by a high proportion of oversized oil paintings on canvas. These remarkably large canvases are as typical of Venetian painting as the frescoed mural is of Florentine or Tuscan art. Quite apart from the size involved, it is always risky to remove a painting from the setting to which it has become acclimatized over a period of, say, four hundred years, and as any painting that requires removal for restoration is likely to be in a partly deteriorated and possibly weakened condition, the very act of removal may cause it further harm. Lengthy transportation or a brusque climatic change may do irreparable damage. The Superintendent was making use of the Villa Garzoni at Pontecasale near Padua because of its proximity to Venice, for the similarity of the climate and, above all, because of its size. The villa's vast halls, designed by Sansovino, could easily accommodate the largest Venetian canvases, but due to lack of funds, it proved impossible to install the climatic controls that might have improved a rather makeshift situation. Restorers could simply not work comfortably in unheated halls during the damp Veneto winter. Still the most unsatisfactory elements of all were the distances involved in carrying the paintings first by boat and then by truck to the villa.

Something had to be found nearer at hand. In 1968, when the sorry state of Venetian art was being catalogued in the Superintendent of the Galleries/UNESCO card index, a deconsecrated church building was made available by the municipality of Venice. The main body of the church was to be transformed into a workshop for the photographing and

*opposite* Samples of stone under test conditions in the restoration laboratory of the Scuola Vecchia della Misericordia. In the background, the campanile of the Abbazia.

restoring of the paintings. The abbey church of San Gregorio had been closed since the Napoleonic suppressions. Built in fifteenth-century Venetian Gothic style, it had a single tall nave covered by a beamed roof; there were no side aisles or lateral chapels. The chancel and its two flanking chapels at the east end were lit with tall lancet windows which could be opened to admit the largest canvases, but first the building had to be entirely renovated. The restoration was carried out by the Superintendency of Monuments using extraordinary funds provided for the purpose by the national General Administration of Antiquities and Fine Arts. The American Committee to Rescue Italian Art, CRIA, contributed photographic and X-ray apparatus to the project. German donors made special lighting equipment available while further contributions of technical and scientific equipment were designated for the laboratory created in an adjacent building. The British Italian Art and Archives Rescue Fund, under the chairmanship of Sir Ashley Clarke, former ambassador in Rome, arranged for the National Gallery of London to design a scientific department with the British fund donating much of the material required. The British fund also underwrote the salaries for three years of an assistant chemist and a photographer, and further early contributions were made by Italia Nostra's British section and by the Nederlands Comité Geeisterde Kunstaden Italie.

It is important to emphasize at this point, and to keep in mind throughout all that follows, that restoration work in Venice is always accomplished under the supervision of the two government Superintendents. It is they alone who decide what needs restoring and how it is to be done. Foreign contributors must leave the final decisions in their hands, although both these offices have always been willing to accept outside advice and have been more than generous in allowing foreign donors to virtually adopt restoration projects as their own. The laboratory at San Gregorio was opened in October 1968 and is still, after almost twenty years, the most important of the city's several facilities for the restoration of paintings.

Among the very first paintings to be restored at San Gregorio was the great series of masterpieces removed from the Madonna dell'Orto, the church where the artist Jacopo Tintoretto was buried in 1594. The entire church was being restored with funds from the Italian Art and Archives Rescue Fund. This two-year project established a high standard for all other such work in Venice and Sir Ashley Clarke decided to move to Venice to supervise subsequent British restoration programmes in the city. He received much well-deserved recognition for his role in the city's preservation, including being made an honorary citizen, but as an initiator and pioneer of great inspiration and energy, the restoration of the Madonna dell'Orto has, perhaps, remained his favourite accomplishment. The church is depicted in the stained glass memorial window commemorating Sir Ashley's life and work in St George's English church in Venice.

Several of Tintoretto's paintings for the Madonna dell'Orto were remarkably large even by Venetian standards, two of them rising from the choir stalls to the very top of the tall Gothic vaulting in the chancel. Scaffolding had to be built in front of each in order to prepare them for removal from the church. Their damaged and deteriorated surface was covered all over with water-soluble rice paper in order to protect it and to prevent paint loss during transportation to the laboratory. The vast, forty-eight-foot-tall canvases were then lowered to the ground with a system of ropes and pulleys. Laid face down, with the paper protecting the painted surface, they were then detached from their wooden frames or stretchers and rolled on to immense wooden drums which were carried in barges to San Gregorio where the paintings were laid out on the floor for relining. This is the operation that requires the great height and space available only in a building like a disused church. The most meticulous part of the procedure involves cleaning old, rotting canvas, accumulated dirt and impacted dust from the back of the painted surface. A great deal will come away quite easily – sometimes even the old canvas itself – leaving the painting intact, adhering only to its original ground of preparation. The strength and durability of sixteenth-century materials is remarkably evident at this stage. So much is written about the fragility and vulnerability of deteriorated paintings and the dangers involved in transportation that this substantial strength seems something of a compensation. However, each painting, of no matter what period, is a separate case study and whereas sixteenth-century materials seem inherently durable, the damage inflicted over long periods, from rising damp in a wall for example, may prove to have been extremely harmful. But normally the rotting canvas comes away in strips, clinging threads can be removed with tweezers and a small vacuum cleaner will lift dust and dirt from the backing. Then the new, in this case gigantic, pre-stretched canvas backing is lowered

---

The campanile of the Madonna dell'Orto, where Tintoretto was buried and which houses some of his greatest masterpieces, now beautifully restored. The church (with its contents) was the first to be restored by British funds after the 1966 flood.

down on to the cleaned back and affixed to the painting with organic glue that penetrates the new backing and soaks through into the painting itself. Small tailors' irons are used to dry the glue. The whole process of relining in this fashion is done with painstaking care. The Venetian authorities have never permitted the use of heavy irons for the drying operation as they have too often been responsible for flattening the impasto of paintings restored in other countries. There has been a good deal of controversy over the restoration of paintings recently, but most critics acknowledge that the Italian policy of caution and what might be described as 'under'-restoring has produced excellent results with no perceptible damage. Of course, relining is not necessarily considered controversial and what is done during the actual cleaning process will vary considerably from painting to painting.

The careful analysis of the painting under consideration begins when the newly backed work is hoisted upright, fixed to a support and examined inch by inch from platforms on the scaffolding built in front of it. First, of course, the rice paper will be washed away with water, laying bare the deteriorated surface. Photography will be used as one essential stage in the long process of analysis: restorers often insist that black and white photographs taken in strong, raking light will tell them more about the painting's condition than a great deal of sophisticated chemical analysis. Nonetheless, chemical analysis is crucial in determining the composition of the original pigments to be matched.

At San Gregorio the complex layers of ground, pigment and binding agents in the Tintoretto paintings were examined with photomicrographs and a tintometer provided by the British. Once identified the original elements could be isolated from spurious corrections, restorations and layers of discoloured varnishes. One of the most sensitive phases of restoration concerns the identification of the artist's original varnishes and those applied during subsequent restorations. It is now recognized that Tintoretto, among many others, purposefully harmonized the tones of his work with varnishes, yet there is no completely accurate, scientific way of determining where the original sixteenth-century varnishing ends and later nineteenth-century layers begin. In certain radical or excessive restorations of Tintoretto's work abroad, the artist's toning varnish was removed along with the later layers leaving discordant colours, like a bright lapis lazuli blue, all too evident in the restored picture. From the very outset restorers in Venice, working under the Superintendent of the Galleries, avoided this pitfall.

The cleaning and restoration proper can begin once the chemical and photographic analysis of the painting is complete and cleaning solvents are specially concocted for each individual work. When the superficial dirt, earlier corrections or repaintings and yellowed varnishes have been removed, the most seriously damaged canvases may assume a pockmarked appearance. The restorer will then fill in the missing passages with water-soluble paints that can be identified by special photography and easily removed at any subsequent time. It is at this stage that tribute must be paid to the restorer's aesthetic sensibility, because if that quality is absent, mistakes can be made that no amount of technical qualification or scientific analysis will ever be able to disguise.

The restoration of a large Venetian painting will almost always take more than a year to

The imposing Scala d'Oro, so-called because of the stucco work of its classical decorations, recently cleaned and freshly gilded.

The Sala del Maggior Consiglio in the Doge's Palace. Tintoretto's "Il Paradiso", the largest oil painting in the world, has been taken down for restoration.

Two of Tintoretto's 58 oil paintings executed for the Scuola Grande di San Rocco: his circular ceiling painting, "San Rocco in Glory", and his vast masterpiece, "The Crucifixion".

accomplish and some paintings spend up to four or five years at San Gregorio. This was particularly true in the early years of the operation when the wages of the personnel involved, coupled with the cost of heating and lighting the building through the winter, proved too expensive for the budget allocated. In the last decade, and especially since the passage of the Special Law for Venice in 1973, funds have been reallocated and the laboratory now functions on a less precarious basis. The number of paintings restored at San Gregorio is vast and the Superintendency is in the process of preparing a complete catalogue of all its restoration work in the two decades following the floods of 1966-7. In the first ten years, approximately twenty-five per cent of the pictures restored benefited from donations made by the international private committees that began to proliferate in Venice during the 1970s.

Not all the restoration of paintings in Venice is carried out at San Gregorio. There exists a facility at the Accademia delle Belle Arti where, for example, the vast Tintoretto 'Crucifixion' from the Scuola Grande di San Rocco was restored. But apart from this single exception in the San Rocco cycle, the remainder of the fifty-eight canvases painted between 1564 and 1588 were all restored on the premises of the Scuola where a third of the lower-floor meeting hall of the building was partitioned off to create space for a restoration laboratory. The entire operation was made possible by contributions made through the International Funds for

The beautiful beamed ceiling *alla Sansovino*, with gilded cornice and brackets, in the Scuola San Giorgio degli Schiavoni. Three of Carpaccio's splendid narrative canvases illustrate the life and legend of St Jerome.

Monuments, an American fund-raising organization dedicated to the preservation of monuments in all parts of the world. (The Edgar Kauffman Foundation of Pittsburg was the principal donor to the San Rocco project.) It was decided at the outset to remove no more than five paintings at a time for restoration so the visitors to the Scuola could see the majority of the paintings in place throughout the five years of the programme's duration. The restoration team at San Rocco discovered a great deal about Tintoretto's technique, especially his use of glazes, both to build up colours and to alter his compositions. These and other discoveries have been elaborated upon in recent studies by Venetian scholars and summarized in a 1983 guide to the Scuola written by Francesco Valcanover, one of Italy's most distinguished art historians and also Venice's Superintendent of Galleries.

Ruskin described the Scuola Grande di San Rocco as one of the three most precious buildings in Italy because of the great cycle of Tintoretto's painting, but other painting cycles also attracted the restorers' attentions. One of the earliest of these projects was the restoration of a series of eighteen paintings, primarily by Antonio Zanchi, depicting episodes from the history of the Benedictine convent of San Zaccaria. This eighteenth-century cycle is not one of the most famous, but it does typify the Venetian preference for oil painting on canvas in lieu of fresco decoration. This project was completed between 1968 and 1970 with funds from the American Committee to Rescue Italian Art. They also provided for the restoration of twenty of the sixty-odd canvases painted between 1680 and 1704 by Gian Antonio Fumiani, a little-known painter of perspective ceilings. His vast masterpiece in the church of San Pantalon had deteriorated to an appalling degree; not only was the extraordinary composition of vertiginous trompe l'oeil blackened beyond recognition by candle soot and grime, but the joints between the sixty canvases had been sewn together with wire to prevent the ceiling's collapse. The immense scaffolding required to dismantle the 1435 square yards of painting proved almost as impressive as the completed restoration which not only saw the relining and cleaning of each canvas, but the carefully calculated remounting leaving no joint visible from below.

Among the most impressive cycles by a single artist is the famous Saint Ursula series painted by Vittore Carpaccio at the beginning of the sixteenth century. The entire series was sent to the National Restoration Laboratory in Bologna for five years and was reinstalled in the Accademia Gallery in 1986. But not all the recently cleaned cycles of painting were executed by a single artist. The Guide Foundation of New York made contributions through the International Fund for Monuments to the vast restoration programme undertaken by the Superintendent of the Galleries in the Doge's Palace. Beginning with one of the most splendid of the paintings in the great Sala del Maggior Consiglio, 'The Apotheosis of Venice' by Paolo Veronese, the climax was reached with the 1982-5 herculean restoration of the largest oil painting in the world, Tintoretto's 'Paradise', which covers 16,750 square feet or more than a third of an acre of canvas.

---

When architects V. and M. Pastor undertook the restoration of the seventeenth-century ceiling in their drawing-room, they unexpectedly exposed a fifteenth-century ceiling beneath it.

Titian's great masterpiece, painted in 1527 for the Pesaro family altar in the church of the Frari, was cleaned and restored in 1977 with funds donated in memory of Professor John McAndrew.

Much of the painted decoration of Venice's important sixteenth-century buildings, like the Tintorettos in San Rocco or the seventeen Veroneses returned to the Sala del Collgio in the Doge's Palace in 1985, was set in heavily carved and gilded wooden framing suspended from structural beams as ceiling ornament. These immensely heavy, ornate ceilings often have to be repaired and regilded before the restored canvases can be reset in them because their iron or wooden supports tend to suffer from corrosion, woodworm or simple rotting. Painting on wooden panels will often show the effects of similar deterioration, as in the case of Titian's great masterpiece, 'The Assumption of the Virgin' which, in 1974, was treated for

84

Donatello's painted and gilded wooden statue of St John the Baptist was carved for the chapel of the Florentine merchants in the church of the Frari.

woodworm in the Frari church in a special laboratory constructed with the financial help of the America-Italy Society of Philadelphia. Otherwise wood seems to endure relatively well in Venice. The 1973 restoration of Donatello's painted and gilded wooden statue of St John the Baptist, financed by Save Venice, Inc., was particularly meticulous because of the high quality of this great fifteenth-century masterpiece. The statue's painted surface badly needed cleaning, but otherwise the object was structurally quite sound. Andrea Brustolon's ornately carved woodwork for the pulpit and ceiling of the Levantine Synagogue in Venice's Ghetto was restored in 1973 by Save Venice, Inc. and also proved to be in a relatively healthy state.

The Schola Spagnola, synagogue to the Sephardic community, is one of the sights of the Ghetto with its prayer hall lavishly restored by Baldassare Longhena.

And the wooden pilings of Venetian foundations have proved remarkably, almost miraculously, durable while roof beams survive much better, as they should do, than their terracotta tile coverings or the brick walls into which they are set.

Some of the most alarming examples of deterioration are found in other types of ceiling decoration than those used in the sixteenth and seventeenth centuries. For the curved, light-weight frescoed ceilings, fashionable in the eighteenth century, the Venetians used extremely thin struts in combination with hemp cord. These delicate iron supports easily corroded in

The Ca'Rezzonico, begun by Baldassare Longhena and completed by Giorgio Massari, is now a museum of Venetian eighteenth-century decorative arts.

the salt air while the hemp often rotted in the relatively ill-ventilated space between the ceiling and the roof. In fact, all the materials employed in these frescoed ceilings seem particularly perishable and the restoration of one of the largest examples, Crosato's great masterpiece in the Ca'Rezzonico, took fully two years to complete.

In Venice, ornamental ceilings of every period were always suspended from the beams fundamental to Venetian construction. Masonry vaulting is, as Jacopo Sansovino discovered to his discomfort in 1537, impracticable in a city where buildings inevitably settle and subside

and the close-laid beams of Venetian functional-ceiling construction were designed to bear the stress of this uneven settling. The eighteenth-century taste for vaulted frescoed ceilings was satisfied with ingenuity: reeds were plaited and woven together to make a large, light-weight and flexible matting that could be suspended from the beamed ceiling and curved to imitate the shape of vaulting. The undersurface of this matting was then smoothed over with a plaster ground in preparation for the final fresco decoration which was applied by the artist standing, or lying, on top of the tall scaffolding erected below. Fresco painting is an extremely durable medium when applied correctly and cleans quite easily, as has often been demonstrated in Florence, but when the support system used at Ca'Rezzonico was laid bare by opening up the floor above, the evidence of deterioration was terrifying. Both iron struts and hemp cord supports had often simply rotted away, leaving the whole mammoth composition hanging by a thread, as it were. The final restoration was a triumphant success; likewise the cleaning of the Tiepolo frescos in the Church of the Gesuati, restored with French funds, and the restoration of another Tiepolo ceiling, financed by the Kress Foundation, at the Church of the Pietà.

Such a brief account can only hint at the number and complexity of problems encountered in the restoration of painting in Venice and barely does justice to the contribution made by the thirty or so international private committees involved in these projects. However, the restoration of paintings, even when it concerns some of the world's greatest masterpieces, is only a small part of the preservation of a city like Venice. If all the great paintings surviving in Venice were to be destroyed tomorrow, Venetian art would still be well represented in museums and collections scattered throughout the rest of the world. But the restoration of paintings alone will never solve Venice's problems any more than the problems of London or New York could be solved by the cleaning of the paintings in the National Gallery or the Metropolitan Museum of Art.

At the same time, it is precisely the spectacular results obtained from cleaning and restoring Venice's paintings that have helped draw the world's attention to the broader issues at stake in the preservation of the world's most beautiful city. Fund-raising committees have been formed in many countries and have collected millions of pounds, francs, dollars and marks to achieve these spectacular results. By mid-1985, foreign committees had contributed more than eleven million dollars to restoration work in Venice. In 1967 alone, the donations exceeded one and a half million dollars while today, almost twenty years later, as many as twenty-six committees are still actively raising funds to preserve Venetian monuments and works of art. Inflation may diminish the real significance of these figures, but paintings have been saved even if we lose sight of the original cost in man hours, technical obstacles and the practical frustrations encountered daily. It took five years to restore Giovanni Bellini's magnificent San Zaccaria altarpiece partly because of the difficulty in obtaining the right shade of lapis lazuli with which to match the colour of the Virgin's robe.

Many of the funds donated over the past two decades have been raised in response to problems that have emerged during the course of restoring works of art and monuments in Venice. This means that restoration work in Venice is in a state of constant expansion. The

---

*opposite* The seventeenth-century Palazzo Mocenigo at San Stae, with its Guarana frescos newly restored, has only recently been opened to the public.

Behind the early Renaissance façade of San Zaccaria lies one of the oldest churches in Venice. Dating from the ninth century, it was the burial place of several early Doges.

The east end of the church of San Zaccaria. Note the contrast between the Gothic tracery and Alessandro Vittoria's classical tabernacle on the High Altar. The ceiling painting is by Pellegrini.

The remarkable late fifteenth-century wooden ceiling in the church of Santa Maria della Visitazione on Zattere was panelled with 58 portrait busts of saints and prophets by artists of the Umbrian school.

Superintendent of the Galleries clarified the goal of this larger aim when he wrote in the 1983-4 'Genius of Venice' exhibition catalogue, 'Whereas in the past there was an elitist and haphazard approach [to conservation], in that only works of the highest quality were restored, now there is a systematic plan, based on research carried out in 1968 and financed by UNESCO, to conserve all the works of art of the historic centre of Venice and the islands.' But paintings were not the sole concern of restorers working in Venice in those early years after the floods.

# Relief: Churches Repaired

THE PROCESS OF RESTORING deteriorated paintings opened up entirely new fields of rescue work, involving the preservation of the fabric of the buildings in which these treasures were housed, and this stimulated the interest and support of many of Venice's most loyal benefactors. The hundred churches, thirty convents and twenty Venetian *scuole* included in the 1969 card index were among the first to receive attention from the Superintendent of Monuments. One of these, the Scuola Grande di San Giovanni Evangelista, was adopted by the first of the American fund-raising committees, the International Fund for Monuments. They had become interested in Venetian monuments in 1967, working in collaboration with the CRIA, and as the decade long restoration of the Scuola Grande was nearing completion, they established an office in the building as headquarters of their Venice Committee. But long before that could be done, the building had to be consolidated in virtually every detail. The roof required extensive repair for a start and all the major sustaining walls had to be reinforced against the buckling caused by subsidence, iron tie rods and steel bands being used at different points to bind the building together. Then the heavy baroque altar in the upper-floor meeting hall had to be propped up and reinforced from below as its immense weight was weakening the entire structure of the building. The Scuola had been constructed on a relatively soft site and subsequent sinking meant that the ground floor was usually awash during an *acqua alta*. The floor was taken up and its foundations relaid while the bases of the columns were left standing in small wells created by the newly raised floor. A pumping system was installed to prevent the accumulation of water under the new flooring after the *acqua alta* had subsided. The ground-floor walls were also sawn through to permit the insertion of a lead damp course. Another part of the building required quite separate attention. The early Renaissance architect, Mauro Coducci, had designed a handsome monumental staircase for the brethren of the Scuola on the side of the building flanking a canal and large lesions appeared in the canal wall caused by the severe subsidence of the heavy, marble-embellished construction. The erosion of its foundations was not as severe as proved to be the case at the Gesuiti, but there was still a

93

The early sixteenth-century cupola of the church of San Rocco, stripped of its leaded sheathing, reveals a deteriorated structure of rotting beams. *(Photograph kindly provided by the custodian of the Scuola Grande di San Rocco.)* Consecrated in 1508, it was rebuilt and enlarged 200 years later.

danger that an entire flank of the building was slowly slipping into the water. Only in 1977, after all this structural work had been attended to, could the marble and stucco ornamentation be restored and the paintings of the upper hall sent to San Gregorio for relining and cleaning.

By this time a great number of important buildings were under restoration, but in this first decade after the 1966 floods they were mostly churches. Later on foreign committees began to show a certain reluctance to raise funds only for ecclesiastical monuments and there developed a tendency to favour other types of building that might appeal to a wider range of patrons. In the meantime, the British Italian Art and Archives Rescue Fund carried out an exemplary restoration at the Madonna dell'Orto and in 1971 the Venice in Peril Fund was formed as its successor. Under Sir Ashley Clarke's guidance, both British committees chose to restore churches that were of pre-eminent artistic or historic interest, but they concentrated on churches situated in poorer districts, far from the average tourist's well-worn path and with scant means at their disposal for repair and maintenance. It was part of British policy not only to restore each church in all its artistic details, but also to render it a sound building for parish use. In other words, altars and paintings were taken care of along with roof repairs and damp-proofing for the walls, but there would also be some sort of heating system installed for the winter and a new electrical system to provide good lighting, and the organ would be put in order as well.

The comprehensive restoration of the Madonna dell'Orto in 1968-9 was repeated for San Nicolò dei Mendicoli in 1972. As this church had always been in a somewhat perilous state, it had been rebuilt many times and already incorporated structural devices intended to consolidate the building. Indeed, when Venice was severely shaken by the violent earth

94

Between 1765-71 the Venetian architect Bernardo Macaruzzi completed the third phase of building for the church of San Rocco with an elaborate Baroque-style façade of Istrian stone.

tremors of the 1976 Udine earthquake, the restorers must have been made aware of the durability of this most unstable of Venetian buildings. The restoration programme was completed in five years with the Superintendency's budget providing for the repair of the roof. The Superintendent of the Galleries was in charge of the restoration of the church's wooden statuary in the newly equipped laboratory at the Ca'd'Oro.

Other private committees also adopted churches to restore. No fewer than six different groups contributed to the restoration of monuments and works of art in the immense Franciscan church of the Frari. The International Fund for Monuments assigned church-building projects to each of its several fund-raising chapters: their North Carolina committee

95

helped to repair the Frari bell tower while a St Louis committee raised money for work in Santa Maria dei Derelitti and the Washington DC chapter devoted its resources to the fine seventeenth-century interior of Santa Maria del Giglio. Also through the International Fund for Monuments, the Kress Foundation virtually adopted the overall restoration of the church of the Pietà, popularly known as Vivaldi's church from the composer's forty-five-year-long tenure as choirmaster to the Pietà hospice. When the Pietà was rebuilt in the mid-eighteenth century, the architect designed the nave as a musical auditorium and whereas the restored church today serves only occasionally as a parish church, it has proved a perfect venue for chamber music concerts.

---

*below* The rood screen at San Nicolò dei Mendicoli, restored by Venice in Peril in 1972, was created from older elements as a structural brace for the nave and sanctuary of the church.

*opposite* (above) The Ca'd'Oro, one of the most beautiful Gothic buildings in Venice. Vandalized in the nineteenth century, restored twice over in the twentieth, it is now a museum devoted to fifteenth- and sixteenth-century arts; (below) the view it commands of the Grand Canal.

Work in progress at the Ca'd'Oro laboratory. Equipped by the Italian Art and Archives Rescue Fund, it specializes in the restoration of small-scale works of art, particularly sculpture.

*opposite* (above) Part of the Giorgio Franchetti collection displayed in the newly restored and reopened gallery at the Ca'd'Oro. Franchetti designed the mock Renaissance chapel in the background to house Andrea Mantegna's masterpiece, "San Sebastiano"; (below) a late fifteenth-century sculpture by Tullio Lombardo (1455-1532) receives the finishing touches of cleaning in the stone restoration laboratory at the Ca'd'Oro.

---

The IFM Los Angeles chapter restored Venice's former cathedral, the handsome Palladian-style church of San Pietro in Castello, a project which stretched out over several years. It even involved installing a small foundry furnace in the belfry of the fifteenth-century, marble-sheathed bell tower in order to repair the old church bells. The fine eighteenth-century organ was also restored and the IFM subsequently sponsored a series of organ concerts at San Pietro, as had been done in other Venetian churches where eighteenth-century instruments were in need of repair. These organs themselves were the survivors of an earlier programme of repair or restoration.

Organ music had always been a great tradition in the Venetian Republic. The ranking musician of the ducal court and church was not the choirmaster, but the organist of San Marco. Throughout the sixteenth century, the greatest Venetian artists – Bellini, Titian, Veronese and Tintoretto among others – decorated many church organ lofts and protected the pipes against dust by providing magnificently painted organ doors, many of which still exist in situ. Nonetheless the original organ mechanisms deteriorated with age and the great eighteenth-century organ builders of Venice simply gutted the organ cases so that not a single instrument survives in a Venetian church from the era of the Gabriellis or Monteverdi.

One of the finest sets of these organ doors, now in the Accademia Gallery, was painted by Giovanni Bellini for the church of Santa Maria dei Miracoli, a small marble-encrusted building which was adopted for restoration by the German committee. Built in late fifteenth-century Renaissance style, this church is unique in Venice in that all its interior and exterior walls are faced with beautifully matched, veined marble slabs. Stone facing in Venice was usually restricted to the façade of a palace or church, hardly ever appearing on side walls and certainly never in the interior: Venetian builders avoided too much stone decoration in order

99

The unusual oval nave of the church of the Pietà, where Vivaldi was long choirmaster, is crowned by Tiepolo's masterpiece in fresco, "The Triumph of the Faith", restored by the Kress Foundation.

*opposite* The church of Santa Maria Gloriosa dei Frari reflected in the waters of a neighbouring canal.

to reduce the risk of excessive subsidence. The weight of building materials was always – and remains today – a prime consideration in Venetian construction.

The stability of the Miracoli was further jeopardized by the fact that one of the side walls actually rose flush from the canal: a circumstance that is rarely encountered in spite of the fact that Venice is a city with so many canals and churches. When the German restorers removed the deteriorated marble panels from the interior walls, they discovered that the brick core of the structure had suffered terribly from the salty canal water permeating much of the wall. The salt rose in the wall through capillary action, reducing the bricks to the consistency of powdered sugar.

Baldassare Longhena's church of Santa Maria della Salute, was built to celebrate the end of the Plague of 1630. It took almost a half-century to complete the building.

The baroque interior of San Stae (contracted form of Sant'Eustacchio) as restored by the Swiss Pro Venezia Foundation with contributions from its government.

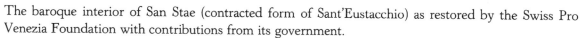

The German restorers were appalled at what they found, but they soon discovered that there was little that could be done about it for the time being as any consolidating agent injected into the disintegrating brick threatened to increase the weight of the canal wall. Science has not yet provided a completely suitable solution to the peculiarly Venetian problems of Santa Maria dei Miracoli. Until such time, the Germans could do no more than replace the marble facing which they realized was no longer merely an ornament as the architects had originally intended, but was actually holding the building upright. Meanwhile the French Comité pour la Sauvegarde de Venise rescued the 'falling angels' on the spectacular façade of Santa Maria della Salute and restored the church to pristine brilliance with the pulverized marble surfacing traditional in seventeenth-century building. White *marmorino* of this sort was also the predominant material used in San Stae's baroque interior, restored between 1977 and 1978 by the Swiss Pro Venezia Foundation of Zurich. This project was remarkable for the participation of the Swiss government as a donor, marking one of the rare contributions made by a government to the restoration of a cultural monument in a foreign country. However, other governments took the cue and recognition of Venice's plight began to be more consistent. The United States government granted exemption from US income tax for donations made to restoration work in Venice and although the British government has never actively encouraged contributors in quite the same way, the Royal Family has set a fine example by attending the inauguration ceremonies of more than one Venice in Peril project.

Paradoxically, the Italian tax structure had actually discouraged private initiative in this field: even after the passage of the Special Law for Venice in 1973, the tax authorities argued that if an individual Italian could afford to donate large sums of money to the restoration of a building in Venice, or anywhere else for that matter, then he must enjoy far greater earnings than he was declaring on his tax returns. Even Venetians who opened their palaces and gave receptions for visiting foreign fund-raising committees were attacked by the authorities with these arguments and obliged to pay increased taxes. The restoration of the exterior of the church of the Redentore was financed by an individual Italian donor who chose anonymity partly for these reasons. The Comitato Italiano per Venezia, on the other hand, initiated a most imaginative restoration of the great Gothic church of Santo Stefano, cleaning all the eighteenth-century side altars to reveal the Venetian love of rich colour in a wealth of rare, veined and dappled marbles.

# Relief: Stonework Conserved

L ONG BEFORE 1974, WHEN SANTO STEFANO'S coloured marble was cleaned, the Venetian Superintendents had begun to concern themselves with the restoration of stone and marble in the city. While often it appeared that only cleaning was required, in fact much of the stonework had crumbled and cracked and it was essential not only to repair the damage already done but to take measures to protect the stone against pollution, often a very much more complicated process than the cleaning of a picture. The poor condition of stone and marble statuary in Venice was taken as evidence of the terrible pollution afflicting the city and the cover illustration of UNESCO's 1969 *Rapporto su Venezia* was a blackened and pollution-ravaged marble head.

Once again the mass media capitalized on the dramatic appearance of the situation without enquiring any too carefully into the facts. They had claimed that Venice was sinking beneath the waves when it was not being flooded by the *acqua alta*, and now they had evidence that the Venetians were living in what appeared to be the most mephitic atmosphere in all of Europe. The petro-chemical refineries were singled out as the villains, despite the fact that Marghera lay a full three and a half miles from the historic centre across open water. In most cities, this three-mile gap would be filled with the pollution from automobile traffic or the oil-fired central heating of houses built on the outskirts. The fact that Venice's prevailing winds, like those of all port cities, are on-shore winds which help keep Marghera's pollutants at bay, was never mentioned in the reports. Nor was any credence given to UNESCO's calculation that sixty per cent of the measurable pollution in the Venetian atmosphere was caused by central heating units in the city rather than by Marghera.

On the other hand, this same UNESCO report did feed the fires of the mounting anxiety over living – and breathing – conditions in Venice with charts, graphs, statistics and photographs of deteriorated marble statuary. It neglected to point out, however, that all the calculations were based on the deterioration of the saccharoidal type of Greek or Carrara marble and applied only to a minute percentage of the city's stonework. Centuries before the advent of industrial pollution, the Venetians had realized how unsuited Greek and Carrara

Typical Venetian waterways and passageways, showing examples of the deterioration of the walls, doors, bridges and carvings in the city. Of the carving at Santa Maria Formosa (above), John Ruskin wrote in *The*

*Stones of Venice*, 'A head – huge, inhuman and monstrous – leering in bestial degradation, too foul to be either pictured or described, or to be beheld for more than an instant.'

marble were to their sea air and climate. It was the corrosive power of the salt sea air that alerted the Venetians to the advantages of another type of stone, *pietra d'Istria*, a micro-crystalline milky white marble, quarried in Istria (today's Yugoslavia) across the Adriatic. Istrian stone stands up well to salt air and is so apparently impervious to water that the Venetians used it as a damp course in their buildings or for the stone steps of water entrances or public quays often immersed at high tide. Again melodramatic photographs of mossy, broken steps are frequently misleading, because the damage is usually due to eroded foundations rather than to any disintegration of the stone. In fact the stone of the step will probably be remarkably intact, even after three hundred years of fluctuating tides, salt corrosion and the growth of barnacles and algae.

Greek or Carrara marble of the saccharoidal type was used only occasionally in Venice for finer carving and sculpture, and the nature of its composition means that there are terrifying illustrations of its deterioration due to corrosion and pollution. The most dramatic case was the highly publicized rescue of two early sixteenth-century kneeling angels carved by Tullio Lombardo and used as the supports of an altar table in the church of San Martino. The November 1966 *acqua alta* thoroughly soaked them with salt water and left them coated with fuel oil. They were among the very first pieces of sculpture to be restored at San Gregorio. After being cleaned, they were placed in specially constructed vacuum chambers and impregnated with silicone resin preservatives to prevent further disintegration. At first, this method of conservation seemed likely to be of limited application in Venice where the bulk of statuary is not free-standing, but usually part of a monumental complex such as a funerary monument or a church façade.

Fortunately most external sculpture in Venice was executed in Istrian stone and not in the more fragile, but finer and crisper medium of Carrara or Greek marble. Even so, the public at large has been given a confused picture of the state of the city's stonework. The parts of any statuary that are not washed clean by rain will attract and accumulate corroding elements, whether they be salts deposited by the sea air, sulphur anhydrides from central heating plants or from the relatively small quantity – given Marghera's immense potential – of industrial pollution that reaches Venice from the mainland. Any of these will eat into the surface of the saccharoidal type of marble at an alarming rate, but Istrian stone has curious characteristics that have helped to preserve it in the long run. The areas of Istrian stone statuary that are not washed white by rainwater will turn black: this is part of the stone's organic nature and not a matter of surface dirt. These black areas also attract a higher concentration of corrosive elements, but the organic blackening serves as a protective skin on the stone. As soon as the Italian authorities realized the implications of this, they became justifiably reluctant to see Istrian stone washed clean until such time as the restorers could also guarantee the stone's future protection.

The foreign press constantly represented the caution of the Italian authorities as the negative attitude of obstructionist bureaucrats. However, the study of stone deterioration financed by UNESCO and the Italian Council of National Research (the CNR) in 1970 emphasized how very little is known for certain about the protection of stone and marble against the corrosion and disintegration caused by modern pollutants. The Italians' caution gained valuable time for the life of Venice's statuary. They were sceptical of chemical preservatives, despite the apparent success in consolidating Lombardo's kneeling angels by impregnating them with silicone resins under a vacuum. After all, silicones were a recent discovery and relatively little was known about their long-term effect on stone. The Superintendents were intent upon preserving for posterity the statuary that had already survived for four or five hundred years. This cautious attitude prevailed when one of the many American committees applied to clean the Istrian stone façade of the church of Santa Maria del Giglio. Although not the work of one of Venice's greatest sculptors, this façade constitutes a unique monument in Venice, if not in all Europe, as it is decorated with a crowd of baroque figures who have no connection with the Catholic church, its saints or indeed even with the iconography of Christianity. Its sole purpose is to glorify the careers and exploits of one generation of Venice's Barbaro family. Over the years, much of the Istrian stone statuary on the façade had blackened, but no one could guarantee the absolute indemnity of these unique works once their protective skin had been removed.

While the Superintendent's caution earned a grudging respect in this case, the foreign committees insisted that he carry out a test cleaning of the Procuratie Vecchie in the Piazza San Marco. A section of one bay of the sixteenth-century building was successfully cleaned, but the Superintendent refused to allow the restoration to proceed even though an Italian insurance company had volunteered to underwrite the costs of the project, maintaining that the cleaning of only one of the Piazza's arcaded ranges would introduce a discordant note in the overall harmony of the square. An American committee then offered to raise funds to finance the cleaning of the remaining arcades, but they were overlooking the fact that cleaning the Procuratie Vecchie façade presented few problems as there was no sculptural ornament to complicate matters, whereas the range opposite was alive to the point of being overburdened with some of the most elaborate ornamental sculpture in the city, partly autograph work of the great seventeenth-century architect and sculptor Baldassare Longhena. And here, too, no one, either foreign or Italian, was in a position to guarantee the preservation of these masterpieces after they had been cleaned.

In the early 1970s, British experts from the restoration department of the Victoria and Albert Museum demonstrated to everyone's satisfaction that they could clean the most delicately carved sculpture without any surface abrasion. This was a remarkable advance in the field of stone restoration, even though it did nothing to solve the twin problems of consolidation and protection of the cleaned stone against pollution in the future. The Venice in Peril Fund then offered to finance a major restoration using these new techniques and the Superintendents agreed upon the so-called Loggetta di Sansovino.

The Loggetta is, in effect, a small pavilion built in 1537 at the base of the bell tower. Its richly carved and ornamented façade illustrates an allegorical programme alluding to the wisdom and justice of the Venetian government on land and sea. It stands opposite the largest and most elaborate entrance to the Doge's Palace and in view of the staircase on top of which the newly elected Doges were crowned. The architect and sculptor, Jacopo Sansovino, seems to have intended its design as a transition between the classical bays of the adjacent Marciana Library and the equally close façade of San Marco with its myriad multi-coloured marble columns.

As soon as the initial cleaning was complete it became clear that colour was the predominant note in the building. But it was in Sansovino's delicately carved bas-relief allegories that the British experts were able to demonstrate their skills and advanced techniques. They used a specially developed tool, shaped like a dentist's drill, for the cleaning. This instrument bombarded the dirt-encrusted surface with a high-velocity stream

The Loggetta was built at the base of the bell tower of San Marco. Behind it rises the Marciana Library. These two masterpieces of sixteenth-century Venetian architecture, both designed in a rich Renaissance style by Jacopo Sansovino, stand together in the Piazzetta.

of minute glass particles which literally vibrated the dirt away without causing any abrasion whatsoever. It was a slow, painstaking process, given the size of the instrument and the precision with which the restorers worked, but the results were splendid. The general cleaning of the rest of the small building was equally successful with the rich red of the Verona marble framing the pristine bas-reliefs and the coloured marble columns complementing the dark green patina of the Loggetta's bronze statuary.

Unfortunately, the conservation of the monument was not quite as successful as a miscalculation in the silicone formula produced a grey, filmy pall which spread over all the

110

coloured surfaces masking the original rich effect. No matter what kind of precautions are taken, this sort of error can always occur. However, the Italian authorities had always understood that silicone resins were irreversible and restorers everywhere now began to appreciate that they might even prove actively harmful in the conservation of stonework. While it is true that these resins consolidate the stone's structure, in the case of much statuary they penetrate only to a certain depth. Then as the summer heat and winter cold cause the stone to expand and contract, the impregnated part of the stone will expand and contract at a different rate from the unimpregnated core and the statue can easily begin to disintegrate from within. None of the qualified experts anticipated consequences of this sort. The National Trust of Great Britain, along with many other similar protectionist organizations, has since forbidden the use of silicone resins in the conservation or consolidation of stone and marble statuary.

It may be wondered that, given their initial scepticism about silicone resins, their refusal to clean certain sculpted façades and their reputation for obstinacy, the Italian authorities ever permitted the restoration in this fashion of Sansovino's Loggetta, one of the masterpieces of sixteenth-century Venetian architecture and sculptural ornament. The answer is a simple one and not without a certain irony. As great a masterpiece as the Loggetta undoubtedly is, it is nonetheless a flawed masterpiece for it was smashed into a hundred pieces when the Campanile collapsed on top of it in 1902. The building that has been restored was actually a pieced-together, reconstituted version of the original, badly in need of cleaning. But even if the project was not entirely successful, its problems encouraged the Superintendents to provide for a restoration laboratory which would specialize in problems related to the conservation of stonework and marble and shortly after its completion in 1974 they acquired the buildings of the Scuola Vecchia della Misericordia for this purpose. Scientific equipment was given to the Misericordia laboratory by the Kress Foundation, among other donors, and research into restoration techniques and methods proceeds apace with actual projects.

The error in the silicone formula was not recognized as such at first and the monument's pallor was attributed to new accumulations of dirt from the polluted air. By this time, however, the city authorities had enacted clean air legislation and all central heating systems were transformed from fuel oil to methane gas. Having thus removed the source of what UNESCO estimated as sixty per cent of the city's air pollution, having no traffic whatsoever, and the advantage of on-shore winds to keep Marghera's pollution at bay, Venice could boast the cleanest air of any city in Europe, though of course this was never mentioned in the foreign press. But the original misconception that air pollution had dirtied the restored Loggetta at least served to emphasize the fact that, in future, simple cleaning or restoration would not be enough, but that funds must be available for maintenance and perhaps even for periodic recleaning. Determining the nature of pollution damage accurately is not just a Venetian requirement especially now that scientists are backtracking on some of their most widely held theories of cause: even concepts like 'acid rain' now stand discredited.

The restoration of the Loggetta also inspired further extraordinary donations to the Venice in Peril Fund which permitted its organizers to approach the authorities and offer to finance another major restoration programme. They expressed the hope that the new project would again make use of the marble-cleaning techniques developed by the British and that the monument restored would be a secular building and not a church. The final choice fell on the Porta della Carta, the great Gothic gateway to the Doge's Palace standing opposite the

Loggetta. A large part of the budget was assigned to the construction of the enormous scaffolding, enclosing it so that the work space inside could be heated and used throughout the winter. The scaffolding was then donated to the Administration of the Doge's Palace, thus stimulating further collaboration between Venice in Peril and the local authorities. This increased sense of co-operation became an integral part of the restoration work itself because the British committee specified that as many Venetian and Italian apprentices as possible should receive training from the Victoria and Albert's experts.

The restoration of the Porta della Carta was, and remains to this day, a triumphant success: the preservatives used to consolidate and protect the rich red Verona marble elements have not in any way altered or veiled the restored depth of hue. Even the Greek marble statues, among the most appallingly deteriorated in the city, were so successfully consolidated that it was decided to put them back in their tall Gothic niches on the gate. The usual caution of the authorities seemed rather less appropriate when it was made clear that these statues, artistically the finest part of the whole, were already too badly ruined to be other than improved upon by the restoration. The final results testified to the accuracy and wisdom of this estimate. The rest of the Porta della Carta, despite the magnificence of its design, would not have been carved by the master himself, but would have been entrusted to his very competent workshop.

In many ways, the restoration of the Loggetta was a unique project, whereas the Porta della Carta inspired an entire series of similar restorations. In late 1985, five years after its completion, large sections of the Doge's Palace were covered with no fewer than three gigantic sets of enclosed scaffolding, each one outstripping Venice in Peril's original contribution. And nearby, the central door of San Marco has been hidden by a similarly enclosed structure for over five years, permitting a restoration team to work on one of the church's most precious, and least-known, sculptural embellishments. The fascia of the church's central arch is carved with representations of the months of the year and allegories of the virtues and beatitudes by an artist often identified with Benedetto Antelami, a sculptor from the Po valley active at the end of the twelfth and the beginning of the thirteenth century. An equally important series depicting Venice's sundry trades and occupations was carved, a hundred years later, on the larger, outer fascia of the main door. An inscription carved in the arch records that Doge Andrea Dandolo ordered a restoration of these bas-reliefs in 1344.

This inscription serves to introduce the one programme of restoration in Venice that has lasted longer than any other in the world. San Marco is undeniably the richest church in Venice and from the outset it required constant care. During the long history of the Venetian Republic and through its three successive rebuildings and enlargements, it never became the city's cathedral but was always regarded as the Ducal Church or Palatine Chapel. Ancient documents make it clear that the Doge had personal charge of its maintenance. San Marco attracted the munificence of the devout as the shrine of the Evangelist, St Mark, and early in its history the church's immense patrimony was placed under the administration of three Procurators, appointed for life. One of the three was responsible for the fabric of the building, but all three – and later, nine – Procurators had a voice in the appointment of the church's Proto or principal and chief architect. The most famous of these, Jacopo Sansovino, was appointed Proto Magister in the year 1529. According to contemporary accounts, he did a great deal to shore up the delapidated building, but today his forty-year tenure is most frequently identified with the mosaics, designed by Titian, Tintoretto and a host of other sixteenth-century painters, that replaced badly deteriorated Byzantine work.

# RELIEF: STONEWORK CONSERVED

The office of Procurator of San Marco still exists as an honour bestowed by the Patriarchate of Venice now that San Marco is, indeed, the city's cathedral. There is also still a Proto who directs a permanent staff of twenty-five specialized workers in a programme of continual maintenance for the building and its treasures. Long before the 1966 and 1967 floods, the Procuratoria gratefully accepted private American contributions to help finance the costly repair of the church's famous mosaics and twenty years later, between 1974 and 1979, the Dumbarton Oaks Center for Byzantine Studies initiated a mosaic study programme that incidentally resulted in further maintenance and cleaning. All of this activity was misrepresented – if harmlessly this time – in the foreign press when a 1984 issue of the *Smithsonian* magazine implied that San Marco's mosaics had just been cleaned and restored for the first time in centuries. The article nowhere mentioned the Procuratoria di San Marco which, in supervising an uninterrupted programme of mosaic restoration active now for at least seven hundred years, must be the oldest permanently functioning restoration organization in the world.

But before considering the most internationally famous – and locally controversial – restoration project carried out under the supervision of the Procuratoria di San Marco, brief mention should be made of two other cycles of Venetian mosaic decoration. Both required urgent work and, in both cases, incidental factors proved to have repercussions just as great as

---

The cathedral church of Santa Maria Assunta at Torcello: part-Byzantine, part-Romanesque, it is here seen across the vineyards that have replaced what was once a thriving city.

the restoration itself. The Torcello project, for example, was the first restoration project to be organized as an international effort from the very beginning, while the single benefactor responsible for financing the restoration of Murano cathedral's splendid mosaic pavement subsequently created a study fellowship programme that has enriched Venice's cultural life immensely.

The formation of the International Torcello Committee was the result of long experience in fund-raising and restoration work and its nucleus comprised the three private international committees which have been most active over the past two decades. The largest of the three, the International Fund for Monuments, maintains a committee office in Venice to facilitate co-operation with the Italian authorities and to handle funds raised by IFM Venice committees scattered throughout the United States. Their Venetian projects have been financed by committees in Washington DC, Los Angeles, St Louis, North Carolina and Minneapolis among many others. Save Venice, Inc., primarily based in Boston, but also with

---

Restored to pristine condition, the early twelfth-century mosaic that covers the floor of the cathedral church of Santa Maria and San Donato at Murano.

# RELIEF: STONEWORK CONSERVED

an active New York chapter, was, from the outset, devoted exclusively to monuments in Venice. Its founder, the late Professor John McAndrew, lived in Venice for six months of the year and, apart from a busy life spent overseeing his committee's many projects, he continued his academic studies with an invaluable account of early Renaissance architecture in Venice. Great Britain's Venice in Peril has always had its own distinctive personality, largely the creation of its president, Sir Ashley Clarke, who has inspired so much restoration work in the city, always pursuing the highest possible standards, and chairman, Lord Norwich, who writes, lectures and broadcasts on behalf of Venice and her problems. The contributions of German and Italian committees were added to this nucleus and the work at Torcello was begun in 1978 with the construction of the statutory scaffolding. Some of this was still in use in the Diaconicon Chapel seven years later, but the results achieved for the building as a whole have fully justified the length of the project.

The restoration of Torcello's mosaics was approached with appropriate caution.

The world-famous mosaics at Torcello undergoing restoration – an international undertaking that has richly repaid the time and money invested.

A private garden on Torcello. The sculptures are muffled in polythene for their protection against the ravages of winter.

Nineteenth-century mosaic restoration in Italian cities like Lucca and, to a lesser extent, Ravenna, were a warning against excess – and specifically against attempting to remove the mosaics and replace them according to specious scientific or mathematical criteria. Glass mosaic tesserae are laid on uneven ground and only the inherited skills of a living craft tradition can possibly recapture the subtlety of the original. In the course of work at Torcello, mosaic scholars from Dumbarton Oaks in Washington DC identified tracts of nineteenth-century restoration on the west wall of the cathedral and, thanks to an examination at close quarters rendered possible by the scaffolding, were able to revise the dating of the mosaics, identifying entire sections as being older than the first mosaics in San Marco. These examinations also revealed that parts of the great Anastasis or Descent into Limbo mosaic had become detached from the wall and were being supported solely by the rest of the composition. The Annunciation mosaic over the arch of the apse was in even greater peril: the foundations of the apse had given way and the apse itself had subsided, breaking away from the body of the building and leaving a fissure in the roof above the mosaic through

116

which rainwater could enter. For the rest, the restoration of the mosaics was a matter of replacing missing pieces, consolidating the plaster backing and washing down the glistening golden ground with specially prepared soap and water.

The mosaic of the Virgin in the apse at Murano distinctly resembles that at Torcello, yet it was the floor mosaic that required radical attention. A great work of art was once again threatened by the instability of construction on a mud-flat building site. In the late 1850s, the Austrians had tried to rebuild the church. Their reconstruction was continued in a similarly heavy-handed, pseudo-historical style by their Italian successors and was completed in 1872. And precisely one hundred years later, a single benefactor offered to finance the cost of taking up the entire early twelfth-century floor in order to strengthen the building's eroded foundations, install insulation and drainage against inundation and repair this great mosaic masterpiece as it was being relaid. The project was begun the following year through the auspices of Save Venice, Inc. and required the collaboration of specialized engineers and mosaic restorers. It was completed after four years and still represents the largest restoration project in Venice ever financed by a single, non-Italian donor. Near the pulpit there is a small bronze square set in the floor. This seals a tube containing a scroll recording in Latin the official gratitude of the authorities, secular and ecclesiastical, to the lady in question. Otherwise, there is no indication of her great generosity to Murano's cathedral. Shortly after the inauguration of the restored church, this same lady established a foundation for study grants to enable qualified students and scholars to live in Venice for a year and pursue their studies.

# The Triumph of the Golden Horses

WHILE ENGLISH AND AMERICAN STUDENTS were being selected and brought to Venice by a foreign-endowed foundation, an Italian corporation sent a single Venetian work of art travelling abroad with truly astonishing results. The tale of the Olivetti Corporation and the Golden Horses of San Marco is part of the story of the Procuratoria di San Marco. In 1974, as the restoration of the Loggetta was drawing to a close and the effects of air pollution on sculpture were being much discussed, the Procuratoria di San Marco decided to accept the advice of scientific consultants and remove one of the four Golden Horses of San Marco for a thorough examination. It was obvious to anyone who climbed up to the church loggia where the horses had stood in the open air for over seven hundred years, with only brief interruptions, that they did require cleaning, even if they did not need all the attentions the scientists were going to lavish upon them. The examination and cleaning of the first horse took three years. In the meantime, UNESCO published a revised edition of its *Venice Restored/Venise Restaurée* catalogue, its cover feature a colour photograph of a decapitated Golden Horse laid out for dissection, as it were, in the Procuratoria's specially prepared restoration laboratory at Sant'Apollonia.

What followed then was a tale full of curious anomalies, not to say absurdities, of the sort that often afflicts a high-minded, if slightly misdirected idealism – a particularly dangerous sort of idealism that cannot be modified for fear of losing face. The Venetians assiduously followed the progress reports in the daily papers because they have always felt an atavistic relationship with the horses, regarding them as a symbol of their city. When the Genoese, the Venetians' arch-enemies, spoke of defeating the Republic in the fourteenth century, they talked of 'bridling the proud horses of San Marco' and not of clipping the lion's wings. Perhaps there is no exact equivalent anywhere else, but one might say that taking the horses down from San Marco would be tantamount to transferring the Statue of Liberty to a museum or sending England's crown jewels to be auctioned off at Sotheby's.

Venice's daily paper, the *Gazzettino*, reported that the scientists diagnosed 'bronze cancer' but then withdrew their diagnosis when they discovered that the horses were hardly made of

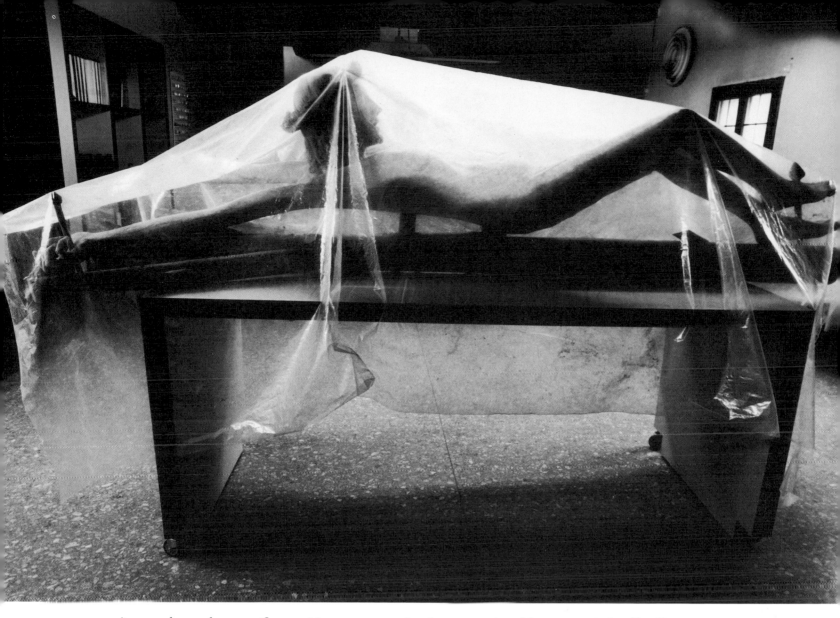

A carved wooden crucifix awaiting treatment in the restoration laboratory of Sant'Apollonia, administered by the Procuratoria di San Marco.

bronze at all, but were almost pure copper. When the authorities decided that the originals should be replaced on the Loggia by copies made of bronze – which presumably would acquire 'bronze cancer' in Venice's supposedly polluted atmosphere – the irony was not lost on the Venetians. Next the scientists sought to discover the cause of the scratch-like disfiguration on the sculpture's surface and if it were in any way related to the apparent losses in the gilding. It was soon decided, however, that the fine web of incised lines was an integral part of the original casting, although none of the experts could explain how it had been done. The casters responsible for the measured bronze copies proved totally incapable of reproducing this distinctive feature. The scientists and art historians then concluded that the horses had never been completely gilded, but that the parcel gilding had been intended, to give their flesh its great liveliness and verisimilitude. Again no one was more puzzled as to how that had been accomplished than those preparing the copies. At vast expense, they had their bronze fascimile lowered into a bath of pure gold of a bright orange hue. The result

119

The courtyard at Sant'Apollonia where a restoration laboratory was prepared specially for the Golden Horses – perhaps the noblest of all symbols of Venetian independence.

proved so unsatisfactory that the orange-gilt copy was whisked away within days of its first appearance on the terrace.

Finally, in the summer of 1977, the newly cleaned, restored and heavily analyzed horse was put on display in special museum rooms arranged in the picturesque cloister of Sant' Apollonia behind San Marco. The horse shone in golden splendour, helped by artificial illumination and all the magic of modern museum display, although the small rooms seemed a bit confining for such a magnificent animal. Many people bought the hefty catalogue with its charts, elaborate calculations, graphs and chemical tables which revived all the spurious, so-called scholarly debate about the origin of the sculpture. Some readers were bemused to see the statue likened, complete with comparative tables of measurement, to the Tennessee Walking Horse when the Lippizaner seemed a much more obvious candidate. Others were surprised to encounter names like Phidias, when the incised pupils of the horse's eyes – a detail never encountered in Greek sculpture – pointed clearly to the statue's Roman origins.

However, all of this debate, both scientific and art-historical, seemed beside the point to the Venetians. The powers that be – and no names have ever been named; no one has ever

120

# THE TRIUMPH OF THE GOLDEN HORSES

stepped forward to take responsibility for the final decision – had decreed that the originals must come down and be protected from Venice's polluted air. Desperate, last-ditch attempts were made to dissuade the authorities, and a number of rather wacky suggestions made – one of them, that electric fans should be installed to keep the polluted air at bay. But as in the story of the Emperor's new clothes, no one pointed out that Venice's air might not be as polluted as it had been in the past, nor did anyone publicly remind the authorities that this magnificent team had survived at least 1600 years exposed to the corrosion of the salt sea air, first at Constantinople and then, from 1205 down to our own day, on the Loggia of San Marco. But the alarm had been sounded, the decision taken, and by way of justification there was even a passage in the catalogue that deplored the potential damage that could be done to the statues by the impact (*sic*) of rain drops. And no one thought to ask where the horses would be displayed once they were taken down.

---

The Golden Horses on display in a small room in San Marco – a location sadly less exalted than the west front of the Basilica which they occupied for seven hundred years.

Before this last question could be considered seriously, the horse vanished. It was off and running, perhaps bearing the banner for Venice, but definitely carrying the Olivetti colours. The lone, restored horse joined one of those innumerable travelling circuses of culture that are so popular today: first it went to London to be viewed by long queues at the Royal Academy, then on to the crowds of New York and Paris. The Parisians also had the opportunity to admire the plaster casts that had been made of the horses when they left Paris in 1814, on the insistence of the Duke of Wellington and Viscount Castlereagh. (The copyists, by now hard at work on their expensive bronze facsimiles, might easily have availed themselves of these casts rather than attempting to reproduce the originals by measurement alone.) Then it was decided to send the restored horse to the city famous for the most polluted air in the world – Mexico City – and finally it was to rejoin all three of its newly cleaned brethren, not in Venice, but in Bonn! Each of the museums involved made handsome profits from displaying the horse and the Olivetti Corporation must have covered its expenses as well. But if any of this money was intended to benefit Venice or even the horses themselves, the Venetians never heard of it.

When the Four Golden Horses finally returned to Venice, they were put on display in a small building next to the church, but the San Basso hall could hardly compete with the large spaces and dramatic settings that had been devised for the sculptures abroad. Large halls are virtually non-existent in Venice and the only suitable space for their display, on historical grounds, might have been within the precinct of the Arsenal where they were first brought from Constantinople in 1204 as trophies of war. But the Arsenal's buildings, including the delapidated Tana or hemp-weaving shed, one of the largest unbroken spaces surviving from the Middle Ages, all belong to the Italian Navy and thus represented a conflict of jurisdiction. It is basically this that has determined the whereabouts of the horses today. They belong to the church, and more particularly to the Procuratoria di San Marco, so they are displayed in a small room in San Marco which can only be reached by climbing one of the steepest and narrowest staircases in the city. They are effectively lit and displayed, but the room is cramped and the ventilation is poor. As yet there are no modern climatic controls to guarantee an even temperature. Nor has anyone installed electric fans, not to blow the pollution away, but simply to keep the air circulating in an enclosed space and prevent the kind of corrosion caused by human perspiration and carbon monoxide exhalations that have obliged the authorities at Lascaux and at Karlstein in Bohemia to close the famous caves and the treasure chamber to visitors forever.

The Olivetti sponsorship of the horses pioneered industrial, business and banking patronage of culture and the arts in Venice, although their initiative had been anticipated to some extent by the RAI, the Italian broadcasting corporation which bought and thoroughly restored the great Palazzo Labia in the 1960s and has since sponsored frequent free chamber music concerts in the ballroom decorated with Tiepolo's famous frescos of the life of Cleopatra. Today, temporary exhibitions, concerts and performances at the Venice Opera House are often underwritten by local and national business concerns. When Mrs Peggy Guggenheim died in 1979 and left her house and her collection of modern paintings to be a

---

*opposite* The Palazzo Venier, once Peggy Guggenheim's residence, still houses her collection of modern paintings and is regularly open to the public as the Guggenheim Museum.

*above* Tiepolo's great *trompe l'oeil* frescos in the Palazzo Labia, now the showpiece of RAI, the Italian broadcasting company. *(By kind permission of RAI)*

*opposite* The Regata Storica, an annual gathering of colourful craft, with the Rialto Bridge in the background.

---

museum in Venice, the new administrators organized the collaboration of Italian banks, businesses and the local and regional authorities. This remarkable co-operation has proved a huge financial success: a considerable contrast to the days when Mrs Guggenheim herself sold catalogues to defray the expenses of opening her house to the public. Even the traditional Venetian festivals of the Redentore, held on the third Sunday in July, or the Regatta Storica on the first Sunday in September, now receive subsidies or assistance from spaghetti manufacturers, insurance companies and Vermouth distilleries.

There seems to have blossomed in Italy a cultural-commercial alliance that is almost as vast as America's military-industrial complex. The most impressive of these interventions in Venice has been the recent arrival of Fiat, the huge Turinese car manufacturer which, through the Agnelli Foundation, has acquired the vast eighteenth-century Palazzo Grassi and intends to develop its former function as a gallery and museum for temporary exhibitions.

The mid-eighteenth-century façade of the Palazzo Grassi, restored by the Agnelli Foundation to house an art exhibition centre. It was inaugurated in Spring 1986 with a show dedicated to Italian Futurism.

Originally organized by a group of Venetian businessmen and industrialists, the cultural programme of the Palazzo Grassi saw the first showing anywhere of Picasso's Picassos, followed by an important series of exhibitions culminating in the 1984 Biennale, dedicated to Vienna's Secession Movement. In 1985 the Agnelli Foundation, backed by all the resources of Fiat Engineering, began the complete remodelling of Palazzo Grassi in order to equip it with the most advanced security installations for art exhibitions. The first exhibition under their auspices, staged in 1986, was dedicated to the Italian Futurist Movement. At the same time, Avv. Gianni Agnelli and the Aga Khan, who in 1985 acquired the Venice-based CIGA hotel chain, asked to have their racing yacht *Azzurra*, the new Italian challenger for the America's Cup, christened in the Arsenal dockyards.

126

# Building for the Future

L ONG BEFORE THE OLIVETTI CORPORATION led the way to commercial
participation in the preservation of Venice, local groups organized on the model of the
foreign committees had adopted monuments in the city for restoration. Whereas the
individual Italian donor might come under attack by the tax authorities for any conspicuous
generosity, contributions could be made on a limited basis through a bona fide organization
without excessive fear of fiscal reprisals. Besides their caution and comparatively restricted
means, the local Italian restoration projects were characterized by an increasing interest in the
preservation of secular buildings. Church buildings had been a real priority in earlier days
because the church had lost the means to maintain, support and defend itself in the hundred
and fifty years since the Napoleonic suppressions, and the consequent impoverishment had
caused severe deterioration and dilapidation. However, donors both at home and abroad
began to feel that church buildings in Venice were capable of absorbing unlimited oblations.
The shift of emphasis might also be explained by the increasing secularization characteristic
of the twentieth century. In 1984, the Cardinal Patriarch of Venice, enjoying an unrivalled
episcopal primacy and prestige in Italy, found only one candidate for ordination in his entire
archdiocese.

In any case, the restoration of Venice's secular monuments was a welcome turn of events,
following on from projects initiated by foreign committees: Venice in Peril's restoration of
the Loggetta and the Porta della Carta; the French restoration of the Procuratoressa Venier's
delightfully decorated eighteenth-century gambling rooms in the Merceria; the Dallas, Texas
Friends of Venice restoration of a carved and gilded baroque ceiling in the Palazzo Pesaro; the
entire *piano nobile* floor of a great sixteenth-century palace restored in 1970 with German
contributions to house the Deutsches Studienzentrum in Venedig, a unique institution that
provides hostel accommodation for qualified fellows as well as concert and lecture rooms and
a reference library; and the 1977 Swedish-financed restoration of the Scuola di San Fantin's
Istrian stone façade.

In 1973 two Italian organizations adopted major secular monuments for restoration. The

The long, curving prospect of Palazzo Pesaro shows one of the very few side walls of a palace in Venice faced with Istrian stone. The cleaning of the stonework was completed in 1985.

*left* The restoration of the courtyard in the Palazzo Pesaro which houses Venice's Museums of Modern Art and Oriental Art. The handsome wellhead was designed by Baldassare Longhena (1598-1682).

*right* The restored courtyard, looking towards the land entrance to the palace and the *portego* or gallery hall windows on the upper floors of Palazzo Pesaro.

---

Società Dante Alighieri, an international Italian cultural institute, raised funds in Italy and abroad to restore the triumphal-arch entranceway to the ancient Venetian Arsenal. It was an appropriate choice as Dante had visited the Arsenal in 1312 and been inspired by what he saw in that extraordinary medieval industrial complex to create some of the *Inferno*'s most vivid imagery. The marble entrance gate was, in itself, an exceptionally important monument, being the very first Renaissance-style building in Venice. But the Società Dante Alighieri did not simply limit itself to the restoration of a single architectural masterpiece: they opened offices in adjacent rooms, lent them by the Naval authorities, and initiated a series of Italian language instruction courses for foreigners. Their lecture rooms are also available to visiting lecturers and foreign students such as those of the Pre-University and Warwick University groups from Great Britain and University of Virginia architecture students from the United States. In 1985 the Società Dante Alighieri sponsored a photographic exhibition devoted to the phenomenon of the *acqua bassa* or excessively low tides. A collection of horrifying photographs illustrated the damage done to building foundations by the wake of motorboats

*above* The façade of the Palazzo Pesaro, a beneficiary of the increased interest in secular restorations that marked the seventies.

*right* The richly carved façade of the Palazzo Pesaro on the Grand Canal took about a century to complete. The recent cleaning and consolidation of the building has taken more than three years.

---

as well as showing the more insidious harm caused by soil erosion or the deterioration of piling exposed to the air. The local interest in this exhibition demonstrated the way in which public opinion in Venice has been made aware of the complexity and extent of Venetian problems.

There is almost an evolutionary pattern in the story of Venetian restoration that begins with the initial alarm over flooding and sinking, continuing through the cleaning of paintings and the repair of church buildings and turning then to the conservation of stonework and the larger problems of atmospheric pollution. All this concern for Venice, both on the local and the international scale, is just now, in the late 1980s, reaching a climax of increasing preoccupation with Venice's little understood natural environment, the lagoon. But long before these latest problems can be tackled – or even assessed with adequate preparation – the city's secular buildings and monuments still require attention.

Just as the Società Dante Alighieri was beginning its work at the Arsenal in the remote Castello district, another Italian group, Venezia Nostra, adopted the Rialto Bridge in the very heart of the city for restoration. This project lasted four years and involved the complete re-

Restoration work on the Istrian stone balusters of the upper floor balconies of Palazzo Pesaro.

*opposite* The triumphal arch forming the entrance to the Arsenal, erected in 1460, is Venice's earliest Renaissance building. The battlemented wall is Gothic; the more ornate statuary was added in the seventeenth century.

roofing of the double row of small shops built on top of the bridge. Its most spectacular aspect, as far as the Venetians were concerned, involved erecting scaffolding underneath half the bridge's span (i.e., still allowing Venice's water buses to pass) in order to clean the accumulated grime of *vaporetto* smoke from the Istrian stone sheathing of the arch. While the Rialto Bridge was still under scaffolding, Venice's Rotary Club celebrated its golden anniversary with the restoration and regilding of figures on the Clock Tower in the Piazza San Marco. And even before this, the Banco di San Marco had celebrated its 250th anniversary by regilding Atlas's great globe on the Customs House where the figure of Fortune pirouettes as a weather vane, holding a golden sail. Under the Venetian Republic, the gilding of sculptural

*above* The Rialto Bridge was built in 1588 of brick faced with Istrian stone. The entire structure was cleaned and restored by Venezia Nostra 1973-77.

*opposite* The early sixteenth-century courtyard of the German merchants' emporium and residence at the Rialto now serves as Venice's central Post Office.

details was just as typical of Venice as was the use of rich colour in Venetian painting and architecture, and even through a sirocco summer haze or a Venetian winter fog, gilding enhances those wonderful effects of water-reflected light. The Procuratoria proved particularly sensitive to this when it regilded the angels' wings and saints' halos, giving San Marco's façade something of the glittering appearance it had had when Gentile Bellini rendered its every tiny detail in his great painting of 1494.

Towards the end of the first decade of restoration work in Venice, local and foreign committees began to seek out projects that might generate positive benefits for the city in the long run. They were no longer as satisfied with the relatively short-term, if spectacular, results of cleaning a painting or a bronze horse, no matter how beautiful. Once again Venice in Peril had pioneered this attitude by having its restorers take on local apprentices, a move by which the British hoped to encourage Venice's development as a locally staffed international centre for restoration studies and techniques. The Società Dante Alighieri turned their restoration work at the Arsenal into a permanent educational programme, while the Delmas Foundation study grants enabling scholars to live in Venice and the creation of a German study centre in the Palazzo Barbarigo della Terrazza are other examples of projects designed to generate future results.

In 1977 the Council of Europe's Pro Venetia Viva Foundation established a 'European Centre for Training Craftsmen in the Conservation of the Architectural Heritage', also partly funded with grants from the government of the Veneto Region. The three-month training programme involves the practical application of Venetian skills in stone, brick, mosaic, fresco, glasswork and mirrors, metalwork, terrazzo flooring, stuccowork, painting and

*above* Chasing and polishing a brass sea horse, the traditional ornament of a gondola.

*opposite* (above) The gilded beamed ceiling of the sixteenth-century Palazzo Barbarigo della Terrazza, despoiled in the nineteenth century of its collection of Titians and now restored as the Deutsches Studienzentrum; (below) The Istrian stone treads and brick structure of a Venetian bridge stripped for repairs to the conduits, pipes and wiring of the city's utilities.

---

decoration. The course has been attended by qualified artisans from all over Europe but Venetian craftsmen have recently begun to take an interest in the centre's activities as well and in 1985, two young specialist painters were admitted to the programme. In 1980 the centre's premises were transferred to the island of San Servolo where abandoned hospital buildings were placed at its disposal. Thus it contributes to the preservation of Venetian craft

skills through its training programme while its presence on the island has proved a pilot project for the use of the lagoon's many abandoned islands.

Another project with equally long-term consequences for the working life of the city was initiated in 1976 with the restoration of the *squero* or gondola yard at San Trovaso. The original funding was found in Munich, but since then the project has taken on an international cast and benefited greatly from the municipal authority's exceptional collaboration. Part of the programme offers subsidies for the repair and refitting of the city's gondolas, many of which are now better maintained than they have been at any time since the Second World War. Only five years later, this project to save a Venetian boatyard would have seemed almost superfluous. Life in Venice changed radically in the 1980s and the small boat-building industry in the city centre and on the islands enjoyed a spontaneous revival unparalleled not just since the end of the last war, but since the last century.

While in the last five years there have been significant changes in the Venetian way of life – the revival of rowing as a sport, the rebirth of the Carnival and the arrival of rich Italians to invest in housing in the city – there have also been changes in the Venetians' own attitude towards life in Venice, changes gradual, but nonetheless perceptible. For example, in the past the city's privileged middle-class young often sought to leave Venice as soon as possible to seek a future in cities more consonant with the twentieth century, such as Milan, Turin, Rome or even Florence. Many of these youngsters have returned to Venice disillusioned by modern urban living and their successors in Venice have begun to make greater efforts to find employment and careers in their native city. The possibilities are limited because Venice is really little more than a small town and these are not working-class youngsters who might follow traditional apprenticeships, but those who can afford to do so may prefer to open a boutique or practise a craft on a small scale rather than enter the anonymous ranks of an enormous corporation in a dirty, noisy and dangerous city elsewhere. There are even some, like the scions of two ancient Venetian noble houses, who have managed to pay homage to their ancestors' achievements in modern terms. One of these has revived the Venetian publishing business practised by his family in the seventeenth century while the other has opened a beautifully executed lace museum on Burano to display the work his great-grandmother encouraged in the islands.

One of the local initiatives that has helped change the Venetian's attitude to life in his own city has been the immensely popular and successful Amici dei Musei e Monumenti Veneziani founded in 1976. The idea originated in UNESCO's Venice office and was turned over to a small core of volunteer workers who built up a programme of local cultural visits and lectures. At first, the greatest successes were registered in the field of encouraging and co-ordinating school visits to little-known Venetian monuments and museums. The Amici dei Musei membership also underwrote the cost of producing a descriptive pamphlet as a brief guide to Venice's Museo Storico Navale, for example. Their numbers have increased year by year and some of the most surprising results came from recent guided visits in the city. Palace owners welcomed groups of Amici but were startled to learn that, such was the enthusiasm for these

---

*opposite* The Lucio Orsoni mosaic factory in the Ghetto and the Rubelli velvet factory next to the Madonna dell'Orto, both point to a brighter future for the *centro storico*, whose struggle to stop the drift to the mainland is beginning to show results at last with the revival of local arts and crafts.

visits, they would have to receive as many as four to six groups of fifty people each on several successive days. Over three hundred Venetians signed up to see the public rooms and luxury suites during a guided tour through the Hotel Danieli. The Amici have also sponsored a number of well-attended lecture series.

When, in 1982, the Italian government passed a law favouring private contributions to restoration projects, the Amici dei Musei adopted the high altar in Baldassare Longhena's great baroque church, Santa Maria della Salute. Standing at the mouth of the Grand Canal, this church occupies a special position at the very heart of one of Venice's most characteristic religious festivals, the Festa della Salute, or Festival of Health, which is held every year on 21 November. Just as when it was first celebrated over three hundred years ago, a bridge of boats is cast across the Grand Canal and the entire city, inhabitants of the historic centre and mainland alike, undertake a pilgrimage to the great votive shrine. Stalls outside the church give the event a fairground atmosphere, selling balloons, toys, traditional fritters, pastries and candyfloss as well as the devotional candles that are offered to the Virgin as protectress of health in Venice. The crowds in the church completely fill the space beneath the mammoth dome while masses are celebrated incessantly and even simultaneously at all the surrounding altars. But the principal object of everyone's attention is definitely the high altar with its wonderful baroque statuary representing Venice's patron protectors, Saints Mark and Lorenzo Giustinian, beseeching the Virgin's aid and intercession. On the other side of the altar from the saints, an angel putto chases away a wicked old witch representing the Plague, a perennial threat in the port city. Of course, the Plague no longer menaces Venice: the real threats to Venice's survival come from elsewhere.

The reasons for Venice's deterioration can be sought in the history of a long period stretching back to the collapse of the Serenissima Repubblica in 1797. The twentieth century has tried to find remedies to preserve the city for the future – not always successful. The idea behind the creation of Marghera in 1917, for example, was to bring back prosperity, yet this well-intentioned initiative almost provoked the city's ruin. On the other hand, the greatest natural disaster to strike in this century, the 1966 flooding, inspired an international concern that can be credited with our chances of seeing Venice safe in the future. The city we see now is not too different from the Venice whose government Napoleon destroyed almost two hundred years ago, and eighteenth-century Venice was not physically much different from the city Tintoretto had lived and worked in two hundred years before Napoleon's advent. With a cautious and careful programme of restoration, calculated according to Venice's natural time scale and not rushed by our own twentieth-century criteria, we may well hope to see the city and its art preserved for a similar span in the future.

The entire story of the attempt to preserve Venice in the latter half of the twentieth century has continued without interruption: what Count Cini did to restore the island of San Giorgio Maggiore in the 1950s is still being done today – in 1984, the international private committees restored more than thirteen major monuments and works of art. Britain's Venice

---

*Pages 140-1* The upswept curvature of the gondola was a modification introduced in the traditional design by the Tramontin *squero* or boatyard in 1921.

*opposite* The boardroom at the Palazzo Reale, Venice office of the United Nations Educational, Scientific and Cultural Organization (UNESCO).

in Peril completed the restoration of Oratorio dei Crociferi situated in the northern quarter of the city which had been closed to the public for almost twenty years. Save Venice, Inc. has offered funds collected in America for the cleaning of sundry paintings while the Minneapolis chapter of the International Fund for Monuments financed the repair and consolidation of the Scala del Bovolo, a unique and picturesque spiral-shaped external staircase built behind the Palazzo Contarini near Campo Manin. It is quite amazing that this international interest in Venice is still so very much alive after fully twenty years. More than once in the last two decades, the chairmen of various fund-raising committees thought that they should discontinue their operations, reasoning that no one could go on asking for contributions indefinitely. And they frequently pointed out, too, that even their most faithful supporters would be reluctant to contribute further when the Italian government was apparently doing so little. But all of that has changed. The Italian government has begun to do more than the private committees ever believed it would or, indeed, could. The reopening of the Giorgio Franchetti collections in the Ca'd'Oro in 1984, after fifteen years of closure, is perhaps a symbol – although a very superficial one – of the government's commitment to the future of Venice's art and monuments. And in that same year, 1984, foreign donors contributed almost half a million dollars – or a billion lire, to make it sound even more impressive – to the government's restoration budget, while the overall total expended by the private committees in two decades reached over ten million dollars.

On the other hand, since the passage of the Special Law for Venice in 1973, the Italian government has spent over forty million dollars on the recent restoration of more than seventy monumental buildings in the city. And in 1983 the budget was increased to anticipate the appropriation of well over a billion dollars for the realization over many years of the *Progettone* or Mega-Project to install moveable barriers to close the lagoon's sea entrances against the invasions of *acqua alta*. There is virtually no point in comparing these sets of figures save to indicate the respective scales of the different undertakings. The restoration of works of art and monuments which has been the primary concern of the international private committees, working in collaboration with the Superintendents of Galleries and Monuments, is one thing; an attempt by the national government of the Italian Republic, in collaboration with all the other levels of government concerned, to resolve the question of Venice's survival as a viable city in the twentieth and twenty-first centuries is something of quite a different order.

But, in fact, the two concerns are inextricably bound together in the sense that were it not for the foreign initiative taken after the 1966 and 1967 floods and pursued with such persistence down to the present day, it is doubtful that the Italian government would ever have recognized the need for a Special Law like that enacted in 1973. After all, many of the Italian Parliament's Deputies and Senators were elected by constituencies whose cities also boasted a tremendous wealth of artistic treasures urgently requiring restoration and

---

Before and after restoration: on p.144, the ceiling of the Oratorio dei Crociferi with Palma il Giovane's cycle of paintings as they used to be and, on p.145, as they now are after the continued efforts of several private committees, Venice in Peril among them.

The Teatro della Fenice: once owned and operated by descendants of the noble families who built it in 1791, the theatre is now public property and is maintained and subsidized by the Italian government.

conservation. For many years, Italy's political representatives saw no reason why Venice's treasures should be favoured over those of Florence, Siena, San Gimignano, Pisa, Assisi, Orvieto, Rome, Ravenna, Ferrara, Viterbo, Volterra, Pienza, Montepulciano, Spello, Spoleto, Gubbio, Bologna, Parma, Mantua, Verona, Vicenza, Bergamo, Pavia, Milan, Como, Loreto, Pesaro, Rimini, Cividale, Turin, Genoa, Lucca, Urbino, Ostia, Naples, Salerno, Amalfi, Paestum, Lecce, Palermo, Siracusa and Agrigento, to mention only those Italian towns and cities with three-star sights. But as the restoration projects of the international private committees laid bare the complexity of Venice's problems and drew the world's attention to the city through their own efforts and the interest of the mass media, the Italian government was gradually obliged to reconsider its position and recognize that Venice was indeed unique among Italian cities, not just for the beauty and incredible circumstances of its setting, but also for the degree of its deterioration. The government also came to understand that flooding and sinking were simply another aspect of the city's dilapidation and that the solutions proposed to revive Venice through industrial prosperity were becoming a more serious threat to the city's survival than had ever been posed by the worst years of her century and a half of poverty, abandonment and neglect.

As if to reinforce this awakening concern on the part of the Italian government, the years of economic recession in Italy revealed tourism to be the nation's single largest industry. And as far as Venice was concerned, this tourism was becoming increasingly cultural in tone. People visited Venice to see what they had read about in the papers: the paintings that had been cleaned, the buildings that had been restored. For years, too, they wanted to see whether or not Venice was really sinking, see if they'd have to wear wading boots to cross the Piazza. The day-to-day problems of coping with both the curious and the serious visitors to Venice could be left in the hands of the local government, but the national government finally understood that it had to protect what remained of an extraordinary national – and, some people were even insisting, international – treasure.

The terms of the Special Law were bound to change the very nature of twentieth-century Venice, but not quite in the way anyone could have foreseen at the time. The Law originally provided for immense amounts of money to be spent on the city, but first the extent of the physical damage had to be determined before it could be decided who was going to spend the money and on what. Even now there is no complete agreement on all the points raised by these definitions. In the meantime, the foreign press has taken the Italian government to task for the slowness and apparent inefficiency of its bureaucratic mechanisms, going even so far as to accuse it of mishandling the funds appropriated for Venice. In this they showed a total ignorance of international financing at the government level. Nonetheless, two British journalists wrote a book on the subject, based on an entirely erroneous interpretation of the facts. In the event, this briefly became a best seller: still the only account of the Venetian Republic's history was Horatio Brown's work and the moment was approaching when almost anything written about Venice in English would find an interested public.

Even though the necessary bureaucratic mechanisms are still incomplete, since 1973 the amounts of government money available for Venice have been augmented by further appropriations and the provisions of the extensive refinancing act passed in 1983, and a great deal has been done. Among other things, in 1969 the government accepted the recommendations of the CNR, the Council for National Research, which had established its Laboratory for the Study of the Dynamics of Grand Masses in the Palazzo Papadopoli. The

# BUILDING FOR THE FUTURE

CNR determined that Venice's accelerated subsidence was being caused by the removal of fresh water from the water table lying beneath the bed of the lagoon. Marghera's industrial plants had been drawing off this water to cool their machinery and engines and under the Special Law, the government apportioned funds for the construction of an aqueduct to supply those needs. When the aqueduct was built, the government ordered all access to the Venetian water table sealed off. This operation was completed with commendable speed and within only three months and against all scientific and statistical probability, the Venetian water table had entirely replenished itself. The government was given the credit for stopping the accelerated subsidence that had so alarmed the entire world ten years earlier. Venice is now no longer sinking.

# Venice's Lagoon

BEFORE THE ENACTMENT OF THE SPECIAL LAW shipping traffic, directed either to Venice itself or to the industrial port at Marghera, entered the lagoon through the northernmost of its three entrances to the Adriatic and crossed through the city up the Giudecca Canal. The Law prohibited large freighters that might be loaded with inflammable material from passing through the centre of Venice and, as an alternative, provided for the dredging of a deep-water shipping channel that would lead from the lagoon's middle entrance at Malamocco directly to the industrial zone. Conservationists launched a series of protests, pointing out that the dredging of a deep-water channel across two separate tidal basins in the lagoon might have disastrous consequences for a body of water so notorious for its tendency to shoal and silt up. There proved to be many justifications for their objections but they came from unexpected sources and in the meantime, the great machinery of authority, backed by the incontestable might of appropriated public funds, proceeded with the project, giving no second thoughts to the consequences. The channel was marked out, dug and dredged in a die-straight line from the Malamocco sea entrance direct to the mainland, there turning north along the shore, crossing into the lagoon's northern tidal basin and finally reaching the Marghera industrial zone.

In the first year, there were rumbles of protest from the ship captains who found that, because the channel had been laid out in a dead-straight line without any reference to the lagoon's natural currents and flow, they had to battle for hours to keep their heavily loaded ships inside its narrow limits. The ship owners began to protest against the channel, too, because the new route took twice as long as the old one. And their costs had soared because the heavier ships had to be under tow for the entire length of the longer journey. Then, too, the lagoon began to shoal and silt up, just as the conservationists had said it might, although the silting did not appear quite where they had expected it, but rather in the very path of the channel itself. The authorities were obliged to commission, with a tremendous expenditure of public money, the construction of special dredging ships for what was euphemistically

150

An unusual view of Venice, seen from the lagoon south of the island of the Guidecca. Left to right, Santa Maria della Salute, the Redentore, the campanile and Basilica of San Marco and the Doge's Palace.

called 'routine maintenance' of the shipping channel. Seven gigantic dredgers worked twenty-four hours a day for twenty-two months to clear a path that nobody wanted to use. In the meantime, cargo shipping returned to the city where it has been ever since, once more passing through the centre up the Giudecca Canal. The exaggerated depth of the shipping channel was supposedly justified as attracting supertankers to the port of Venice-Marghera, but the planners ignored the fundamental reality that the upper Adriatic itself is too shallow for supertankers even if the channel could be maintained at an adequate depth.

One of the Special Law's most positive provisions blocked the expansion of the Marghera

151

industrial zone and specifically the plan to enlarge the facilities with the creation of a second zone. The necessary space was conveniently at hand in the sense that an infinite amount of land can always be reclaimed from the lagoon. In fact, this reclamation had already been accomplished by 1973: a large area had been blocked off with a perimeter of piling and the enclosed space filled in with waste, rubbish and earth. By this time, however, the government had become aware of the degree to which the lagoon had progressively been diminished by land reclamation over the previous one hundred and fifty years. The French first and then the Austrians had filled in the channel between the monastery islands of San Cristoforo and San Michele to create the city's cemetery island. The Austrians had enlarged the island of Sant'Elena tenfold to provide parade grounds and barrack space for the cavalry regiments billeted in the city. After the Unification of Italy, the area around the railway station was extended and then, just after the turn of the century, vast areas were reclaimed to expand Venice's railhead into a dock and storage area known as the Stazione Marittima. Following the Second World War, an entire island was created at the western edge of the Giudecca to provide space for private housing, and another at the end of the road bridge became a gigantic car park and bus terminal island, the Piazzale Roma. This area was subsequently enlarged even further by the dumping of so much rubbish into the lagoon nearby that a third large island formed: now the Tronchetto, the city's open-air car park, the city authorities have

The industrial port of Marghera seen from the Giudecca Canal – still used as a thoroughfare for heavy cargo shipping despite an attempt to divert it outside the city.

Seen from the lagoon, the factories and refineries born of entrepreneurial genius that were to have rescued the city from poverty.

recently been considering plans to increase the size of this zone again in order to bring still more cars into Venice. And further north in the lagoon, the shore line was extended out into the water to create a facility large enough to handle the largest jet aircraft, the Marco Polo Airport. Yet even today, more than ten years later, no authority has been found willing to dismantle the piling perimeter that surrounds the vast reclaimed area. If the piling were removed, the tides would eventually reduce it by erosion and once again extend their spread over a greater area within the lagoon.

While all the uncontrolled reclamation was under way and the second industrial zone was being planned, a change in the practices of the lagoon's fish nurseries further reduced the surface area washed with the daily tides by as much as one fifth. Fish breeding in the lagoon still follows many of the ancient practices and traditions. In winter, fish migrate to the lagoon's warmer, shallow waters, following winding channels to the western mainland shore, and nets can be strung across these channels to prevent their return to the sea. The resulting net-enclosed areas are called Valli da Pesca or Vales for Fishing. The captured fish are fattened for market throughout the winter season and in the summer, when the lagoon waters

153

become too warm, the fish move back towards the cooler, deeper waters of the sea but are blocked by the nets, so can be caught and conveniently taken to market. Since the war, Valle owners have taken to replacing the perimeter nets with earthwork dykes or solid barriers which, of course, require little maintenance and act as an effective deterrent to would-be poachers. But while this is an eminently practical solution, it has reduced the lagoon's surface area. Re-opening the Valli da Pesca to the tidal flow might help restore some of the lagoon's lost equilibrium, especially where the *acqua alta* is concerned. It is an issue that is fraught with problems, however. Many of the Valle properties have changed hands since the war and the real owners often prefer to hide behind holding companies and anonymous corporations. They have resorted to these subterfuges not necessarily because they wish to avoid re-opening their Valle to the sweep of the tides, but because these stretches of lagoon may well, according to the law, prove to be part of the public domain. Thus despite the fact that the Special Law specifically declares Venice's entire natural environment to be of national interest, nothing has been done about the Valli, even though many people – including Italia Nostra, Venezia Serenissima, Estuario Nostro and the World Wildlife Fund – believe that they may hold the key to reducing the frequency of flooding in the city.

Another of the problems posed for solution by the Special Law was the use of moveable barriers that could be raised up to close off the sea entrances during the *acqua alta*. Opposition to these barriers came first of all from the shipping companies who feared greatly increased costs if their ships were held up for twelve hours or twenty-four hours or even longer while the *acqua alta* ran its course. The text of the Special Law therefore had their interests in mind when it made the incredible provision that barriers should be constructed to close only two of the three sea entrances to protect the city from the *acqua alta*. This amazing piece of nonsense did not go unobserved by the Law's critics who realized that the middle or Malamocco entrance was being left open to give permanent access to Marghera via the shipping channel. They anticipated that once the moveable barriers had closed off the rest of the lagoon to the high water, the only way to keep the Malamocco entrance viable would be to construct a dyke along either side of the shipping channel and thus isolate it from the different water level, effectively destroying the very nature of the lagoon altogether. In addition, scientists have affirmed that any division of the lagoon will inevitably result in an increased number of *acqua alta* floodings in the city.

The most serious doubts about closing the lagoon entrances come from fishermen and Venetians who have made the lagoon their life's study. They point out that, no matter what scientists would like to believe, we know relatively little about the way the lagoon functions and what we do know clearly indicates that it is quite unpredictable. Even scientists have had to swallow this unpalatable truth where the *acqua alta* is concerned. They no longer regard the *acqua alta* as a tidal condition, solely dependent on the moon's gravitational attraction at certain seasons and times of the day. The Mediterranean has virtually no daily tide at all

---

*opposite* (above) Deep-water channels run alongside the factory and refinery sites of the industrial port of Marghera on the mainland shore of the Venetian lagoon.

(below) The harbour of San Pietro in Volta on the Lido is crowded with trawlers and fishing boats.

although there is some tidal fluctuation in the upper Adriatic, primarily because its narrow shape and shallow depth make its enclosed cul-de-sac configuration more sensitive to the moon's pull. When a low-pressure area builds up over the lower Adriatic, usually at that point where the shallow bottom drops off into the Mediterranean's greater depths, the waters are pushed into the upper part of the sea. These low pressure build-ups are usually accompanied by the sirocco, Venice's prevailing wind that blows from the south-east up the length of the Adriatic, a warm, ennervating wind that picks up humidity in its passage across the Mediterranean. Paradoxically enough, it also brings with it sand from its source in the Sahara: Venetians may find it deposited with the dew the morning after a bout of humid sirocco weather. Tourists often complain of the way the sirocco humidity makes July and August temperatures uncomfortable, but in fact it blows throughout the year in Venice.

The combination of the sirocco and a heavy low-pressure area over the lower Adriatic may be sufficient to cause a spell of *acqua alta*. And if this combination happens to occur at the times of the moon's maximum gravitational pull – i.e., during the autumn or spring equinox – then an *acqua alta* is almost a foregone conclusion. However, it must be kept in mind that all this depends initially on the weather. In other words, if the wind is blowing from another quarter, say from the north-east, in early November, there will probably be no *acqua alta* at all. Alternatively, if there is a steady build-up of *acqua alta* conditions and then the wind changes direction, the threat will disappear completely. When it does come, the *acqua alta* acts like a tide, flowing into the lagoon for six hours and ebbing away for six. This means that for at least half of this twelve-hour period, no matter how high the maximum reached, the Venetians can walk dryshod everywhere in the city. The relative instability of weather patterns and the time it takes to create the right circumstances for an *acqua alta* in the upper Adriatic mean that the average cycle of high water will last for a couple of days at most. But again, if the wind changes, the entire cycle and all its consequences will vanish in a trice.

Even the most hardened devotees of scientific certainty will admit that no one can yet predict where a wind is going to come from next, how long it might blow from that direction, or with what force. And yet all of these are factors which determine the presence of the *acqua alta* in Venice. The scientists are not even sure whether a mathematical model of the lagoon's behaviour or a physical model constructed some fifteen years ago near Padua at a cost of half a million dollars and never used since, or else a more detailed study of the lagoon itself would be most useful in establishing the degree to which modifications to the lagoon might relieve the city of excessive bouts of *acqua alta*.

As always the example of the Venetian Republic, which survived in this setting for over a thousand years, might be instructive; but few have time for the long and complicated lessons of history. The Republic's powerful Magistrato alle Acque, guided by patricians who had jurisdiction over the lagoon and all its navigable channels, could not legislate without first consulting a specially convoked council of eight fishermen, whose superior first-hand experience of the lagoon would always be respected. In many ways, the history of the Venetians and their lagoon could serve as a guideline to today's administrators and scientists alike. After all, the issue at hand is essentially an old one: *plus ça change, plus c'est la même chose*.

Originally the Venetian lagoon was a river delta, a swampy marsh area into which three major rivers and sundry smaller tributaries emptied. The delta was separated from the

156

The practices of the fishermen in the controversial Valli da Pesca are currently under heavy attack from the conservationist lobby.

greater depths of the Adriatic by the Lido, a long, thin, shoal-like littoral which in the past was broken by at least nine different openings to the sea. The river currents and the tidal counter-currents passing through the delta carved the canals and deeper channels from between the mud flats characteristic of this shallow body of water. The rivers also brought silt with them and in the fourteenth century, large stretches of the northern lagoon silted up, becoming a stagnant breeding ground for the malarial mosquito. Entire islands like Torcello were abandoned, never again to recover their flourishing prosperity. Indeed, with solid building materials at a premium in this marshy setting, the richer and more important buildings on the islands were simply dismantled and their brick and stone reconstructed elsewhere in the lagoon. One can find marble blocks with Latin inscriptions and the thin *altinella* brick of Roman building that have migrated in this way over the centuries from Roman Altinum on the mainland to Torcello and then to the historic centre of Venice itself. But as intriguing as all this is in retrospect, the facts behind it represented an unmitigated disaster for the lagoon dwellers. Torcello's population, which had reached forty thousand in the Middle Ages, today stands at forty-five, and of the hundreds of buildings that once stood on the island, only a dozen or so remain. The vineyards and artichoke fields are peppered with archeological debris, the fragments of foundations belonging to the many monasteries, convents and church buildings of the past.

The fifteenth-century government of the Venetian Republic decided to adopt a radical solution to preserve the health of the entire lagoon. It was a herculean undertaking that entered into its final phase in the early sixteenth century, but before it could be achieved, there emerged in opposition to the government's plan a faction which maintained that large tracts of land should be reclaimed from the lagoon for agricultural purposes. This was the period in Venice's history, just after the fall of Constantinople to the Turks, when Venetians worried about their excessive dependence on imported foodstuffs: supplies that had to be shipped great distances across waters which were now in the hands of the hostile Turks. The government was already actively encouraging its patriciate to invest in farming the hinterland, closer to the lagoon – an episode in Venetian social and economic history that would, in the next generation, give rise to Andrea Palladio's great farm villas on the mainland. But in the meantime, a great deal of marshland had already been reclaimed in the area between the lagoon and Padua and the lagoon itself began to seem ideally suited to large-scale reclamation and farming. Fortunately for the survival of the Venice we know today, the agriculture lobby did not gain the upper hand. The maritime traditions of the Republic still prevailed in the councils of the government and the Arsenal shipyards remained the industrial heart of the city.

In the early sixteenth century, Cristoforo Sabbadini (1487-1560) noticed the encroachment of reed beds in the southern lagoon, advancing towards his native Chioggia. Thoroughly alarmed, he applied the full force of his intelligence and his powers as a writer to convince the government of the Republic that their original project for the northern quarter should be extended over the entire lagoon: all the river mouths should be diverted to empty outside the lagoon and in addition, several of the sea entrances on the Lido should be closed in order to reduce the number of openings through which the tides could flow with increased force. This newly concentrated force would propel the tide waters as far west as possible, effectively enlarging the lagoon; ebbing over a greater distance and through fewer openings to the sea, the tides would scour the channels deeper. Only thus could the health of the lagoon be guaranteed. In the words of a proverb of Sabbadini's day, '*Gran laguna fa gran porto*' – the larger the lagoon, the greater the port. The government adopted Sabbadini's recommendations and concluded the gigantic task of diverting the river mouths in the following century. Six major entrances to the sea were closed by the simple expedient of constructing palisades and allowing the currents to fill them in with sand and however simple this might sound, the operation depended for its success on an intimate understanding of the sea currents and tides.

Reducing the lagoon through reclamation was out of the question and the problem did not arise again for over four hundred years. For those four hundred years the lagoon was, just as Sabbadini hoped it would be, a healthy body of water and a healthy setting for the great city that prospered and was protected in harmony with its surroundings. The Venetian government well understood the import of what they had accomplished by following Sabbadini's advice. In 1553 the Magistrato alle Acque inscribed in marble an admonition to future generations that remains valid to this day:

# VENICE'S LAGOON

VENETORUM URBS
DIVINA DISPONENTE PROVIDENTIA
AQUIS FUNDATA
AQUARUM AMBITU CIRCUMSEPTA
AQUIS PRO MURA MUMITUR
QUISQUIS IGITUR
QUOQUO MODO DETRIMENTUM PUBLICIS AQUIS
ANFERRE AUSUS FUERIT
HOSTIS PATRIAE JUDICETUR
NEC MINORI PLECTATUR PEOMA
QUAM QUI SACROS MUROS PATRIAE
VIOLASSET
HUJUS EDICTI JUS RATUM PERPETUVMQUE
ESTO

(The city of the Venetians/with the aid of Divine Providence/was founded on water/enclosed by water/defended by water instead of walls./Whoever in any way dares damage the public waters/shall be declared an enemy of the State/and shall not deserve less punishment/than he who breaches the sacred walls of the State./This edict is valid forevermore.)

It is important to remember that since Sabbadini's day, the lagoon of Venice has been, to all intents and purposes, a man-made body of water. It is no longer the river delta that nature made; indeed, it is now almost entirely a salt water basin. The Venetian lagoon provides the perfect illustration of man's ability to alter the natural balance of his surroundings to suit his own purposes without destroying any fundamental harmony in nature. But such alterations must be made with great caution, based on a profound understanding of the forces of nature and allowing her to play the greatest part in bringing these changes about.

Almost everyone concerned with protecting Venice from the *acqua alta* today has assumed that the erection of moveable barriers to close off the sea entrances constitutes an ideal, if not the only possible, solution. Such barriers would be raised up from the sea bottom to isolate the lagoon whenever an onslaught of *acqua alta* were predicted. Of course, the flaw lies hidden in the unknown quantity of meteorological changes, and the clauses of the Special Law highlighted another weakness by providing for the installation of the barriers at only two out of the lagoon's three sea entrances. But the arguments in favour of the barriers have been presented with such conviction, and backed with such an authoritative array of pseudo-scientific data, that this strategy has assumed the character of a foregone conclusion. The basic concept of the project has been approved with little dissent from official quarters, although not so much as an opinion has been sought from the only engineering firm in the world that has already installed such barriers. Of course, the problems solved by the moveable flood barriers on the River Thames are only superficially similar to those of the lagoon, just as the Dutch experts who have been consulted on lagoon matters from time to time derive their experience from a situation diametrically opposed to that of Venice. The Venetians actually want the sea to come into their city, even though they may not want too much of it at a time.

When the shape and scale of the moveable barrier project first became known, there was a considerable outcry – an outcry from those with the sort of personal, lifelong experience of

159

the lagoon that the ancient Republic would have respected and an outcry now echoed by all the major committees organized for the preservation of Venice, including Italia Nostra and the World Wildlife Fund. The cause for the alarm is not the barriers themselves and the function they would perform, but the gigantic, permanent earthwork structures that must be erected both inside and outside the lagoon to hold them in place. These enormous breakwaters, dykes and barriers extending far into the lagoon and out to sea will definitely change the flow of tides and currents, provoking consequences of unpredictable proportions.

In the recent re-financing of the Special Law, over 150 million dollars was assigned to the various competent authorities to study the feasibility and the possible consequences of what has become known in the city as the *Progettone*. This more cautious approach has been welcomed by the conservationists on the one hand, but criticized as a terrible waste of the taxpayers' money on the other. Given the number of authorities involved, the Venetians expect several years to pass before sufficient evidence is gathered on which to base eventual recommendations. There are even some who hope against hope that time and inflation will do their worst and that the *Progettone* will meet the fate of that other utopian scheme of 1858 for an international exposition centre on the Riva degli Schiavoni, never realized for lack of funds. Meanwhile, the condition of the lagoon seems to be deteriorating at such a rate that long-range questions concerning the *acqua alta* and the gigantic barriers recede into a remote and irrelevant insignificance. The very first report (issued in four volumes in November 1985) drawn up by the experts consulted for the *Progettone* concluded that at present practically nothing is known for certain about how the lagoon works.

The farmland that drains into the lagoon is often infected with chemical fertilizers and pesticides; the petro-chemical refineries of Marghera discharge tons of chemical substances every day; and the Venetians themselves make their own contribution to this massive poisoning with the chemical detergents and plastics that are part of everyday refuse. It has also been discovered that the city's canals, which have not been drained or dredged for two decades at least, now contain high concentrations of poisonous metals, zinc and mercury, from effluents and also from metal objects often dumped by irresponsible Venetians directly into the canals. The deposits excavated from the Rio Baratari, drained for the first time in decades in 1985, were unloaded into the water near Murano causing local pollution of alarming proportions.

The result of all this is a burgeoning ecological disaster. In 1984 and 1985 the lagoon bred a superabundance of algae which the currents pushed up against the lagoon side of the Lido. This thick green seaweed has caused the suffocation of millions of small fish whose bodies putrify in the summer sun, and the dying algae itself turns black in the summer heat and produces a stench, redolent of drains, that is really more like the putrid odour of stale water in a flower vase. This is all the more alarming for the curious side effect that causes silver exposed to this fetid air to tarnish in a flash and turn black overnight. Even in the past, when the algae lining the walls of a Venetian canal were exposed to the air by the low tide and dried in the hot summer sun, they produced an odour which tourists assumed was the smell of drains. Venice prematurely acquired an unfair reputation as a smelly, dirty city which it has been hard-pressed to live down. And although such a description is inaccurate still, there is no question that Venetian waters now run the risk, for the first time in the one thousand five hundred years of man's recorded settlement in this environment, of becoming unhealthy.

# Venetian Life Enriched

◄─❀─►◄─❀─►◄─❀─►◄─❀─►◄─❀─►◄─❀─►◄─❀─►◄─❀─►◄─❀─►◄─❀─►◄─❀─►

A S MUCH AS VENETIAN MONUMENTS have been successfully preserved as relics of a glorious past, there is now every hope that Venice's natural environment may be saved by that same combination of international concern and national legislation that has hitherto done so much for the city. The problems involved are immense and they become more complicated both with time and with the increased means available, but although the levels of government and the number of jurisdictions involved seem endless, the Special Law has already achieved a great deal. The fact that more than forty million dollars has been spent on the restoration of some seventy Venetian monuments has already been mentioned. Many of these monuments are palaces of historical and architectural interest, although few if any of them have received attention simply because of those considerations. For the most part they are ancient palaces that have been used, for the last several generations at least, as schools or public buildings. Yet this initiative on the part of the authorities to restore historic buildings that house not museums but law courts (Palazzo Grimani, Palazzo Contarini-Cavalli and the Fabbriche Nuove at the Rialto), municipal or regional government offices (Palazzo Loredan, Palazzo Balbi and Palazzo Flangini-Fini), schools and university facilities (Palazzo Dolfin, Palazzo Cappello-Layard and Palazzo Recanati) and government agencies such as those located in Palazzo Duodo at Sant'Angelo – all this has inspired much restoration in the private sector as well.

Not far from Palazzo Pisani-Moretta on the Grand Canal there rises the splendidly restored early Renaissance, Istrian stone façade of the Palazzo Grimani-Giustinian-Marcello, while nearer the mouth of the Grand Canal, in 1985, after five years of restoration, the scaffolding was removed from the beautiful fifteenth-century Gothic palaces of the Contarini family, one of which the Venetians regard as 'Desdemona's house'. Both these restorations, like that carried out on the interior of the exquisite fifteenth-century Renaissance Palazzo Dario, were financed with private money. The Special Law did offer certain financial inducements to these and other owners, but landlords generally express a slightly caustic evaluation of these incentives. While the authorities promise to reimburse the owner for up

161

Two fifteenth-century Gothic palaces of the Contarini family on the Grand Canal. The wheel tracery balconies of the Palazzo Contarini-Fasan – "Desdemona's House" – are unique in the city.

to eighty per cent of the cost of restoring an historic monument's exterior and even up to sixty per cent for work on the interior, the government sets a ceiling on the cost of working-man hours which is currently about fifty per cent below the actual going rate. And calculations for the eventual reimbursement must be based on the original estimates and not on the final expenditure. Before embarking upon a major restoration project (of, say, five years' duration), it will probably take two to three years to obtain all the appropriate permissions. By the time the work is completed, costs will have risen and inflation decimated the value of the original

162

The restoration of this minor palazzo, which was privately financed, is a sign of the times — a vote of confidence on the part of her citizens in the city's long-term prospects.

estimates. And the owner cannot expect to be reimbursed much less than ten years or so after having submitted the estimates for the original project.

Thus restoration in the private sector has not been inspired solely by government goodwill and promises, but by something much subtler and more impressive, representing a commitment by the city's inhabitants to Venice's future survival. They have been encouraged partly by the sincerity of the world's concern, partly by the government's participation in the preservation of Venice and partly by a cynical but realistic estimate of Venice's potential role

The Palazzo Balbi, now a government office building. Its restoration was made possible only by the generous financial provisions of the Special Law for Venice.

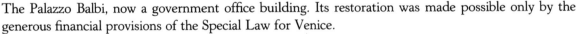

in Italy today and in the near future. First of all, it is now appreciated that Venetian property and its improvement might well prove a sound investment. Venetian real estate is unique. When no fewer than four cabinet ministers stood for election as Mayor of Venice in the 1985 administrative elections, those who had bought houses or apartments in Venice must have realized that their instinct had been a good one. However, it has not been an easy instinct to act on, even for the very rich; nor has it been inspired by anything other than an unfortunate, from their point of view, set of circumstances.

These unfortunate circumstances were general all over Italy, but did not much affect Venice or the Venetians other than by bringing the rich of Italy to make their homes in Venice. Italian newspapers today often describe the 'seventies as the *'anni di piombo'*, the leaden years, with the distinct implication of lead as in bullets. During that decade political

The Palazzo Franchetti next to the Accademia Bridge. Formerly Palazzo Gussoni-Cavalli, it was much restored and enlarged by Baron Franchetti in 1896.

terrorism earned Italy a sad reputation throughout the world and inextricably linked to this tragic phenomenon in the public's mind were the older, better established, but no less violent and murderous traditions of the Sicilian Mafia and the Neopolitan Camorra. All three of these criminal elements in Italy specialized in killing, traded in arms and drugs and, in the 1970s, began to finance their operations through kidnapping. This last activity became a particularly horrific part of life in Italy, especially in the big cities, and for years no one seemed immune from the threat. Many rich Italians began to send their children to foreign schools and universities or to reside abroad themselves, returning home surrounded by the most elaborate security precautions. At the same time, there was a frightening increase in the incidence of street crime of the most vicious sort while the Italian economy was shaken by the effects of worldwide recessions and universal inflation. The government has dealt with many

165

of these problems in different ways and, among other less widely acclaimed successes, has apparently broken the threat of organized political terrorism.

But it was not the Italian government's campaign against political terrorism that changed Venice's prospects for the future. More significant was the introduction of a series of stringent fiscal measures designed to cure Italy's economic crisis and bring a rampant inflation under control. Among the many provisions of these new tax laws was a period of grace during which all Italian citizens could bring back into Italy all their capital invested or banked abroad. From henceforth, any Italian holding so much as the title to a bank account outside Italy would be breaking the law and would be liable to heavy fines and imprisonment. The same Draconic regulations applied to any attempt to export capital out of the country.

Many Italians soon found that the government was in deadly earnest. Important industrialists and businessmen, whose well-known names would once have insured immunity, were now subjected to embarrassing surveillance and even searches at airports and border crossing points, with any cause for suspicion possibly resulting in arrest. The Italian police and the judiciary still enjoy many of the procedural advantages devised under the penal code of the Fascist regime. For example, 'preventative detention' means that a suspect can be held indefinitely without being charged, without even being questioned and therefore without the possibility of bail; he may even be denied access to a lawyer with perfect impunity. Every Italian is aware of the frightening possibilities of arrest and with this threat looming large, even the very rich are now beginning to take the government's exchange controls seriously.

In addition, the government put drastic limits on the amount of money an Italian could take out of Italy for the purposes of a holiday. All of these measures threw the rich Italian back on his own resources. His way of life did not change much except that in Rome, Turin and Milan, as well as in a number of smaller cities, he would always be heavily dependent on the protection of bodyguards and the safety afforded by a bullet-proof limousine. These precautions against kidnapping also extended to his wife, who no longer wore so much as earrings or a fur coat or carried a handbag in the street, and to his children, who had to be escorted to and from school. Yet, even in the more tranquil, safer climate of the mid-eighties, there has been at least one major kidnapping for every day of the year. In these 'major' cases, the ransom demands usually exceed a million dollars, but the general pattern also involves a nerve-shattering period of up to half a year before the kidnappers make their demands known.

Venice has never had a single case of kidnapping, nor are there muggings; even purse-snatching is extremely rare. House-breaking and petty theft are headline events when they occur and only one small branch of a local bank has ever been robbed with something approaching regularity. This particular branch is located on the Zattere, a broad promenade alongside the Giudecca Canal – one of the few bodies of water suited to escape in a high-speed motor boat. But even that does not work very well because Venice, as a port city and well-known centre for smuggling, is full to overflowing with coastguard boats and helicopters that can easily run down even the fastest getaway.

The long and short of all this is that Venice, unlike most cities and even some smaller towns in Italy today, is safe. Rich Italians began to appreciate these unique qualities in the late 'seventies and investing in Venetian real estate became attractive. All the international interest in Venice had made it fashionable to know about the city and the restoration work going on there, and with its relaxed pace, absence of traffic and streets safe from muggings, it seemed the ideal place for holidays or for weekends away from Milan and Rome. By now the rich were beginning to feel the pinch of exchange control restrictions and to be nervous of harassment by customs officials. Italy's traditional vacation spots had lost some of their appeal: Portofino, Port'Ercole and Capri were now overcrowded with daytrippers and even the most secluded spots proved to be no safer than the major cities from the ever-present threat of kidnapping. Industrialists had been snatched from their villas in remote corners of Tuscany while in Sardinia, kidnapping had been a local cottage industry since time immemorial. Venice proved an attractive alternative, particularly as it was less than an hour's flight from either Rome or Milan.

So the rich came to Venice. In 1980 more than half of all the real estate transactions were sales to non-Venetians, yet only three of the buyers in that year were not Italian. In the five years since then, the rich have changed Venice discreetly, though radically, restoring more of the city's fabric than either the government or the thirty or so private international committees. And it is important to emphasize that this 'foreign' invasion of wealth is an exclusively Italian phenomenon: the non-Italian residents in Venice are very few indeed. It has been estimated that only about forty or fifty foreigners from English-speaking countries, by far the largest non-Italian concentration, live permanently in Venice and most of them live in rented accommodation. The rich Italians do not rent but buy, even if the property is intended only as a *pied-à-terre* for occasional weekends. None of them has been interested in acquiring a great palace or even owning and restoring the *piano nobile* of an immense house. No one knows better than they how difficult it is to staff a large house or apartment. They want something small and convenient that can be locked up and safely left empty during the working week in Milan.

The rich Milanese have bought the houses of the poor in Venice, those same small delapidated buildings deserted by the working classes during the terrible depopulation of the city in the 'fifties and 'sixties. The Dorsoduro quarter near the Salute church where, under the Venetian Republic, the very last wooden houses were built in the city, has become the smart neighbourhood *par excellence*. The rich have also discovered what the native Venetians have always known: that Venice is extremely small – only two and a half square miles – and that charming and picturesque areas are to be found scattered everywhere. The Venetians have been quick to profit from this newfound interest in their delapidated housing and the real estate market has soared out of all proportion, well beyond the reach of the natives themselves. Nonetheless, all of this has become an integral part of the story of how Venice has been preserved. Non-Venetians have proved willing to pay a quarter of a million dollars for a small house – the sort foreigners used to call a 'gondolier's cottage' – comprising two or three bedrooms, two baths, a sitting-cum-dining-room and compact services. Terraces may be sought after, but are not traditional in Venice and the terribly restrictive laws governing restoration make it virtually impossible to install a terrace where none has existed previously. Of course, a gondolier's cottage does not actually have any of the rooms described above, particularly not bathrooms, modern or otherwise; nor any plumbing or electrical wiring, let alone central heating, iron safety shutters, solid doors and double locks, or the sort of tile or marble paving to cover a floor that has to be raised and insulated against the threat of an excessive *acqua alta*. But the rich have proved to have the resources and, through their lawyers and architects, the time and patience to apply to all the sundry authorities for permission to put these houses in order. Once the permissions have been granted and old partition walls knocked down, rotting beams might reveal themselves or, as in more than once case, it might be discovered that a room has been enlarged in the past and the beams are no longer firmly set in the walls at all. Time and money will eventually cure all these ills, but the Venetian authorities have never permitted short cuts or tolerated any infringement of their strict requirements.

All of this was demonstrated, very recently, in the case of an extremely rich and prominent lady, a member of one of Italy's most influential industrial families, who bought an attic in Dorsoduro to convert into a mansard apartment. She engaged one of New York's most famous interior decorators, a qualified architect who boasted the even more relevant qualification and distinction of being a native-born Venetian. He made the sundry applications to the authorities and the work began. Scaffolding was erected, the roof tiles and beams repaired, and slowly but surely the conversion of the attic began. Eventually, after three years, the transformation was complete and all was ready for the owner to take up residence. There was only one small hitch. The authorities refused to grant permission for the construction of a staircase by which the lady might actually reach her apartment. And there the question lay, at an impasse, for a further two years. Now, with the permission finally

A wooden 'paper hat' joined the 1985 Vogaloga, the non-competitive boating rally over a twenty-mile course which takes place every year on the first Sunday in May.

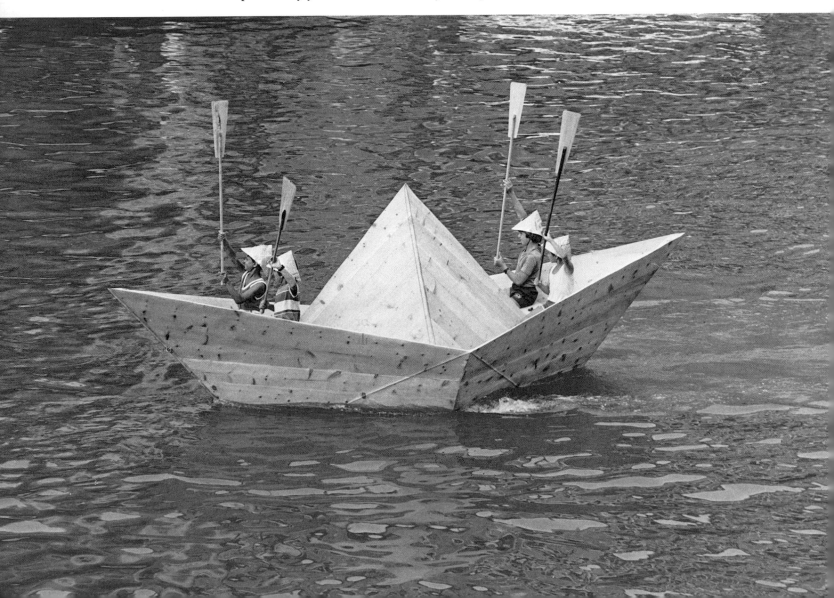

A demonstration of the gentle art of *voga veneta* – Venetian rowing as revived by the city's wealthier professional classes in the eighties.

available, five years after the initial purchase, the work has begun again, this time dismantling much of what was done before in order to accommodate the newly approved staircase.

Despite these obstacles, rich Italians have invested a great deal in Venetian real estate and Venice now has the highest percentage of uninhabited housing of any non-resort city in Italy. Yet much of the city's housing has been saved from abandonment and dilapidation. Although the influx of rich Italians has made it difficult for the Venetians to buy houses in their own city, many of them can share in the financial health this has brought by finding employment as carpenters, masons, engineers, plumbers, electricians, painters and upholsterers. And the new inhabitants have been absorbed into the fabric of Venetian life with unusual and unexpected consequences. For example, rowing in the traditional Venetian fashion, standing and facing the bows, has been borrowed from Venice's fishermen to be practised as a sport by quite a different class. In fact, the fishermen who still row to their nets are becoming few and far between: the majority have opted for the convenience of outboard motors. For a while it seemed that the *voga veneta* or Venetian rowing would disappear altogether and that the only form of rowing sport on the lagoon would be the English sculling introduced in Venice at the end of the nineteenth century by smart rowing clubs like the Bucintoro. But by the 1980s, applications for membership in these clubs had increased fiftyfold as they adapted themselves to the newfound fashion for Venetian rowing. Rich Italians, in their Venetian *pied-à-terre* for the weekend, had taken up the *voga veneta* for exercise, as they might have taken up jogging in other cities. Even more important for the Venetian economy was the virtual rebirth of the small boat-building industry as boatyards at Burano and on the Giudecca began producing beautifully crafted and finished versions of the fisherman's *topo* or the tourist's *sandolo* for the weekend oarsmen. This newly widespread popularity of sport-rowing in Venice gave rise to the Vogaloga, a twenty-mile non-competitive marathon for every sort and kind of water craft, an annual event, scheduled for the first Sunday in May, which has seen up to five thousand participants. Neighbourhood rowing clubs have proliferated in the wake of the Vogaloga with local Venetian businessmen rowing newly built, brightly painted versions of the *caorlina*, a six-oared cargo barge, the sleek *puparin*, a nineteenth-century gentleman's sport rowing boat, or the flat-hulled skiff called the *sciopon*, once used for lagoon duck-shooting in the days of the blunderbuss.

The vogue of sport-rowing has simultaneously preserved a traditional Venetian skill and revived the vanishing craft of small-boat building while the Carnival, an equally recent development, reanimated a season which, only ten years ago, was the time for Venetian restaurants and hotels to close their doors as the staff sought seasonal jobs in nearby ski resorts. To anyone aware of the attention the Venetian Carnival has attracted, it seems incredible that this long weekend of festivity and merriment simply did not exist as such a decade ago. And it is also curious that it was neither the Venetians themselves, nor the recent rich arrivals who were responsible for the revival of the tradition, but rather the youth of the mainland cities of Padua, Treviso and Vicenza among others who, in 1975, decided to come into Venice on the appropriate winter weekend, dressed in homemade fancy dress costumes. All Venice had to offer was a lucky bout of sunny weather and its absence of traffic; the Carnival was a completely spontaneous affair and its instigators came back again the following year, with their friends. By the third year, the municipal authorities realized that they had to assume control, indeed police, an event that might easily get out of hand. But it was precisely Venice's reputation as a safe city that lent itself so well to the merriment and high jinks and Venice's theatrical qualities provided a perfect setting for the new Carnival. Famous photographers began to appear to capture the increasingly elaborate costumes and masks cavorting in such spectacular surroundings. The rich followed suit, at first coming over in droves from Milan to see for themselves, then being entertained by their Venetian friends and acquaintances, and finally attending the lavish balls and parties organized by fashion designers and public relations promoters. In the meantime, the municipal authorities and the Biennale contributed a rich programme of rock bands for dancing in the city squares as well as concert and opera performances at the Fenice.

---

*opposite* Venetian reflections in a showcase full of leather and papier mâché masks for the Carnival.

One of hundreds of boutiques to have capitalized on the success of Europe's latest carnival, supplying the demand for elaborate handmade masks.

*opposite* Santa Maria della Salute at sunset.

---

Carnival has undoubtedly been a boon to the Venetian economy. Venice's hotels are completely booked over the Carnival weekend and it often proves difficult to find a table in a restaurant whether grand or humble. Even after the festivities have ended, Venice profits from its reputation as Europe's new carnival city. There are now hundreds of boutiques selling elaborate and expensive handmade masks while the local bookshops overflow with costly volumes illustrating the costumes of Carnival today.

Of course, the Venetians themselves tend to be bemused by all the fuss, if slightly annoyed and inconvenienced by the invasion of their public spaces, their squares and cafés, and the appropriation of their public transport by what seem to be literally millions of merrymakers. Many of them have adopted a callous attitude towards the supposed economic advantages brought by all these outsiders. Few if any Venetians want to concede that mass tourism contributes anything at all to the city's economy. These changes in the pattern of Venetian life appear to them as so much ephemera. But they are quick to point out that for their children there is still little or no future in Venice, save in tourism, in the small shipping business or in a luxury glass industry floundering in a state of perennial crisis. They appreciate the improvements that have been made, they are pleased that all the art is being cleaned and restored because they fervently believe that their city is the most beautiful in the world. However, they also know that these works of art and monuments have been restored by outsiders, whether they be non-Italians or Roman bureaucrats. They also see that their houses, even the poorest, are now lived in by non-Venetians. They see their city becoming a city of the rich. So Venice has been preserved, but preserved for whom must still seem a pertinent, if as yet unanswered question.

# Index

*(An italicized entry indicates an illustration.)*

Accademia Bridge, 70; *71*
Accademia delle Belle Arti, 80
Accademia Gallery, 38, 83, 99
Adriatic Sea, 11, 23, 25, 51, 150, 151, 156
Aga Khan, 126
Agnelli, Avv. Gianni, 126
Agnelli Foundation, 124-6; *126*
Alexandria, 6
America-Italy Society of Philadelphia, 85
Amici dei Musei e Monumenti Veneziani, 139-42
Anatolia, 11, 17
Antelami, Benedetto, 112
Arsenal, 51, 123, 126, 129-130, 134, 158; *133*
Austria, 20, 38, 47-8, 51, 54

Balkans, 17
Banco di San Marco, 132
Baratari, rio, 160
Barbarigo family, 40
Barbaro family, 109
Basilica of San Marco, 3, 6-8, 36-7, 41, 49, 99, 109, 112-13, 116, 118-23, 134; *6-7, 121*
Beauharnais, Eugène de, 38
Bellini, Gentile, 40-1, 134
Bellini, Giovanni, 89, 99
Benchley, Robert, 1
Benedictines, 59
Berchet, Federico, *49*

Berenson, Bernard, 50
Biennale, 54-5, 126, 172
Bon, Bartolomeo, 18
Britain, 28, 76
Brown, Horatio, 35, 148
Browning, Robert, 1
Brustolon, Andrea, 85
Bucintoro, 170
Burano, 49, 139, 170
Byzantium, 3-4, 10-12, 17; *6, 52-3*

Ca'd'Oro, 95, 146; *97, 98, 99*
Ca'Grande, 46
Ca'Rezzonico, 87-9; *87*
Campanile, 41, 111; *42, 151*
Campo Manin, 146
Campo Santa Margherita, *62*
Canaletto, 57, 66
Carità, 46
Carnival, 170-2; *171, 172*
Carpaccio, Vittore, 15, 83; *82*
Cassiodorus, 18
Castlereagh, Viscount, 123
Cavour, Camillo, 48
Chioggia, 158
Cimabue, 28
Cini, Giorgio, 56-7; *59*
Cini, Count Vittorio, 54-7, 142; *57*
Clark, Sir Kenneth, 35
Clarke, Sir Ashley, 76, 94, 115
Clock Tower, Piazza San Marco, 132
Coducci, Mauro, 4, 93
Columbia Broadcasting System, 29

Comitato Italiano per Venezia, 104
Comité Geeisterde Kunstaden Italie, 76
Comité pour la sauvegarde de Venise, 104
Committee to Rescue Italian Art (CRIA), 28, 33, 76, 83, 93
Constantinople, 3, 11, 17; *6*
Contarini family, 37
Le Corbusier, 69
Corte Seconda del Milion, 3
Council of Europe, 134
Council of National Research (CNR), 108, 148-9
Crete, 17
CRIA, *see* Committee to Rescue Italian Art
Crosato, 87
Crusade, Fourth, 10-12, 14
Customs House, 132

Dallas Friends of Venice, 127
Dalmatia, 17
Dandolo, Doge Andrea, 112
Dandolo, Doge Enrico, 11-12
d'Annunzio, Gabriele, 50
Dante, 129
Delmas, Foundation, 134
Deutsches Studienzentrum in Venedig, 127; *136*
Discalced Carmelites, church of, 52
Doges, 6, 12-14, 18
Doge's Palace, 37, 83-4, 109,

111-12; *12, 13, 14, 15, 16, 24, 80, 151*
Donatello, 85; *85*
Dorsoduro, 26, 167-9
Ducas, Michael, 17
Dumbarton Oaks Center for Byzantine Studies, 113, 116

Edgar Kauffman Foundation of Pitsburg, 82
Ercole Varzi Foundation, *32*
Este family, 12
Estuario Nostro, 155
European Centre for Training Craftsmen in the Conservation of the Architectural Heritage, 134-7

Fabbriche Nuove, 161
Teatro della Fenice, 172
Ferrara, 12, 17
Festa della Salute, 142
Festa Nazionale, 18
Fiat, 124-6
Film Festival, 55
First World War, 51-4
Florence, vii, 14, 17, 23, 26-9, 31, 35, 70-2, 89
Fondaco dei Turchi, 47-8; *48, 49*
Fondazione Ercole Varzi, 31
Fortuny, Mariano, 50
Foscari, Doge Francesco, 18
France, 18, 28, 36-8, 127
Franchetti, Giorgio, 146; *98, 165*
Franks, 11
Frari church, 46, 85, 95; *84, 85, 101*
Fumiani, Giovanni Antonio, 83

Gaggia, Ingegnere, 54
Gallini, Giacomo, 18
Gama, Vasco da, 17
Garibaldi, Giuseppe, 48
*Gazzetino*, 118-19
Germany, 56, 127
Gestapo, 56
Gesuati, Church of the, 89
Ghetto, 85; *139*
Giudecca canal, 150-1, 152, 166, 170; *21*
Giudecca island, 49
Giustinian, St Lorenzo, 142
Golden Horses of San Marco, 118-23; *120, 121*
Gonzaga family, 12
Grand Canal, vii, 47, 60, 142, 161; *20, 63, 97, 162*
Guggenheim, Peggy, 123-4; *122*
Guide Foundation of New York, 83

Hitler, Adolf, 55
Holy Land, 11
Hotel Danieli, 142
Hungary, 11

International Fund for Monuments (IFM), 80-2, 83, 93, 95-9, 114, 146
International Torcello Committee, 114
Ionian islands, 17
Istria, 108; *61, 128, 132, 134, 136*
Italia Nostra, 33, 76, 155, 160
Italian Navy, 123

Jerusalem, 11
Jesuit church, 42-5, 93
John VIII, Emperor, 17

Kress Foundation, 89, 96, 111; *100*

Labia Palace, 123
Laboratory for the Study of the Dynamics of Grand Masses, 149
Layard, Sir Henry, 40-1, 49
Levant, 17
Levantine Synagogue, 85
Libro d'Oro, 18
Lido, 11, 25, 49, 156-7, 158, 160; *19, 50*
Lisbon, 17
Loggetta di Sansovino, 109-11, 112, 118, 127; *110*
Lombardo, Pietro, 4, 40
Lombardo, Tullio, 4, 108; *98*
Lombardy, 17
Longhena, Baldassare, 41, 109, 142; *21, 87, 102, 129*

McAndrew, Professor John, 115
Macaruzzi, Bernardo, *95*
Madonna dell'Orto, 76, 94; *77*
Magistrato alle Acque, 19-20, 156, 158-9
Malamocco, 19, 20, 150, 155
Manin, Daniele, 38, 41, 47
Manin, Doge Lodovico, 17-18
Mann, Thomas, 50
Mantegna, Andrea, *98*
Mantua, 12
Marcello, Contessa Andrianna, 49
Marciana Library, 109; *110*
Marco Polo airport, 153
Marghera, 54, 56, 60, 68, 105, 108, 111, 142, 149, 150-2, 155, 160; *152, 153, 154*
Mark, St, 4-10, 14-15, 112, 142
Massari, Giorgio, *87*

Mediterranean, 1, 17, 155-6
Mehmet II, Sultan, 17
Merceria, 127
Mestre, 54, 67, 68-70
Morosini, Francesco, 37
Milan, 12, 14
Murano, 48-9, 114, 117, 160; *8, 114*
Murazzi, 19-20, 25, 26; *19*
Museo Storico Navale, 139
Mussolini, Benito, 54-6

Napoleon I, Emperor of the French, 3, 17-18, 31, 36-8, 45, 46, 142; *59*
National Broadcasting Company (NBC), 29
National Restoration Laboratory, Bologna, 83
National Trust, 111
Norwich, Lord, 115

Oberon, Merle, 57
Olivetti Corporation, 118, 123, 127
Oratorio dei Crociferi, 142-6; *146*
Ottoman Empire, 17
Otway, Thomas, viii

Palazzo Balbi, 161; *164*
Palazzo Barbarigo della Terrazza, 134; *136*
Palazzo Cappello-Layard, 161
Palazzo Contarini-Cavalli, 161
Palazzo Contarini del Bovolo, 146
Palazzo Contarini-Fasan, *162*
Palazzo Dario, 4, 161; *5*
Palazzo Dolfin, 161
Palazzo Duodo, 161
Palazzo Flangini-Fini, 161
Palazzo Franchetti, *165*
Palazzo Grassi, 124-6; *126*
Palazzo Grimani-Giustinian-Marcello, 161
Palazzo Labia, *124*
Palazzo Loredan, 161
Palazzo Mocenigo, *88*
Palazzo Papadopoli, 149
Palazzo Pesaro, 127; *128, 129, 130, 131, 132*
Palazzo Pisani-Moretta, 41, 46, 161; *39, 40*
Palazzo Pitti, 66
Palazzo Reale, *142*
Palazzo Recanati, 161
Palazzo Venier, *122*
Palladio, Andrea, 52, 59, 158; *13*
Paul VI, Pope, 27
Pellegrini, *91*
Pellestrina, 19

Peloponnese, 17
Piazza San Marco, 20, 25, 29, 109, 132; *25, 42*
Piazzale Roma, 152
Piazzetta, *10, 110*
Picasso, Pablo, 126
Pietà, Church of the, 89, 96; *100*
Pisani family, 41
Polo, Marco, 3
Porta della Carta, 111-12, 127
Pro Venetia Viva Foundation, 134-7
Pro Venezia Foundation of Zurich, 104; *103*
Procuratie Vecchie, 109
Procuratoria di San Marco, 113, 118, 123, 134; *7, 119*
Procuratoressa Venier, 127
*Progettone,* 146, 160
Proust, Marcel, 50
'Provisional Municipality', 18

RAI, 123
Redentore, Church of the, 104, 124; *151*
Regata Storica, 124; *124*
Renaissance, 4
Rialto, 26, 161; *68, 124, 134, 135*
Rialto Bridge, 130-2
Ridotto della Procuratoressa Venier, *44*
Risorgimento, 48
Riva degli Schiavoni, 47, 66, 160
Roman Empire, 6
Rome, 3
Rotary Club, 132
Rubin, Baroness Maria Teresa, 34
Ruskin, John, 4, 46, 47, 82; *52-3, 107*

Sabbadini, Cristoforo, 158
San Baso hall, 123
San Cristoforo, 152
Santa Fosca, 3
San Giorgio Maggiore, 18, 45, 57-9, 66, 142; *2, 57, 58, 59*
SS. Giovanni e Paolo, 46; *45*
San Gregorio, 46, 76-80, 108
San Marco Basin, 66
Santa Maria dei Miracoli, 4
San Martino, 108
San Michele, 47, 152; *46*
San Moisè, 66
San Nicolò dei Mendicoli, 94-5; *96*
San Pantalon, 83
San Pietro in Castello, 8, 99

San Pietro in Volta, *154*
San Rocco, *94, 95*
San Sebastiano, 31-2; *32*
San Servolo, 137
San Stae, 104; *103*
San Trovaso, 139
San Zaccaria, 45, 82-3, 89; *90, 91*
Sansovino, Jacopo, 87, 109-11, 112; *13, 110*
Sant'Angelo, 161
Sant'Apollonia, 118, 120; *119, 120*
Santa Croce, 52
Sant'Elena, 152
Santa Lucia, 47
Santa Maria and San Donato, 3, 48; *8, 114*
Santa Maria Assunta, *113*
Santa Maria dei Derelitti, 96
Santa Maria dei Miracoli, 99-104
Santa Maria del Giglio, 96, 109
Santa Maria della Salute, 41, 104, 142, 167; *21, 71, 102, 151, 173*
Santa Maria della Visitazione, *92*
Santo Stefano, 104, 105
Saracens, 11
Save Venice, Inc., 44, 85, 114-15, 117, 146; *84*
Scala del Bovolo, 146; *42*
Scala d'Oro, *78*
Scaligeri family, 12
Scuola San Giorgio degli Schiavoni, *82*
Scuola dei Nobili, 47
Scuola di San Fantin, 127
Scuola Grande di San Giovanni Evangelista, 93-4
Scuola Grande di San Marco, *4*
Scuola Grande di San Rocco, 80-2, 84; *81*
Scuola Vecchia della Misericordia, 111; *75*
Second World War, 20, 54, 60
Sforza family, 12
*Smithsonian* magazine, 113
Società Dante Alighieri, 129-30, 134
Special Law for Venice, 80, 104, 146-9, 150-2, 155, 159-60, 161
Sposalizio del Mar, 18
Stazione Marittima, 152
Stucky grain mills, 49-50
Superintendent of the Galleries, vii, 70, 72-3, 74, 92, 95
Superintendent of Monuments, vii, 70, 72-3, 76

Sweden, 127
Switzerland, 56

Tana, 123
Teatro Fenice, *146*
Theodore, St, 8
Tiepolo, Giovanni Battista, 41, 52, 89, 123; *100, 124*
Tintoretto, Jacopo, 3, 76-8, 80-2, 83-4, 99, 112, 142; *77, 80, 81*
Titian, 3, 40, 84-5, 99, 112; *84*
Torcello, 49, 114, 115-17, 157-8; *113, 115, 116*
Trevelyan, G.M., 38
Tronchetto, 152-3
Turks, 11, 17, 47-8

UNESCO, vii, 21, 33-5, 74, 92, 105, 108, 111, 118, 139
United Nations, 68
Unites States of America, 28, 29, 127

Valcanover, Francesco, 82
Valli da Pesca, 153-5; *157*
Venezia Nostra, 130-2; *134*
Venezia Serenissima, 155
Venice in Peril Fund, 94, 104, 109, 111-12, 115, 127, 134, 142-6; *96, 146*
Venice Opera House, 123
Verona, 12
Veronese, Paolo, 3, 18, 31, 37, 41, 52, 83-4, 99; *32, 45*
Verrochio, Andrea, *4*
Victoria and Albert Museum, London, 109, 112
Villa Barbaro, 52-4
Villa Foscari, 52
Villa Garzoni, 74
Visconti family, 12
Vittoria, Alessandro, *91*
Vittorio Emmanuele II, King of Italy, 48
Vittorio Emmanuele III, King of Italy, 56
Vivaldi, Antonio, 96; *100*
Vogaloga, 170; *137*
Volpi, Count Giuseppe, 54-6

Wellington, Duke of, 123
World Wildlife Fund, 155, 160

Zanchi, Antonio, 82-3
Zara, 11
Zattere, 166
Zorzi, Alvise, 36